T0311758

Cambridge Elements ≡

Elements in Applied Linguistics
edited by
Li Wei
University College London
Zhu Hua
University College London

METALINGUISTIC AWARENESS IN SECOND LANGUAGE READING DEVELOPMENT

Sihui Echo Ke
University of Kentucky

Dongbo Zhang
University of Exeter

Keiko Koda
Carnegie Mellon University

CAMBRIDGE
UNIVERSITY PRESS

Shaftesbury Road, Cambridge CB2 8EA, United Kingdom

One Liberty Plaza, 20th Floor, New York, NY 10006, USA

477 Williamstown Road, Port Melbourne, VIC 3207, Australia

314–321, 3rd Floor, Plot 3, Splendor Forum, Jasola District Centre, New Delhi – 110025, India

103 Penang Road, #05–06/07, Visioncrest Commercial, Singapore 238467

Cambridge University Press is part of Cambridge University Press & Assessment, a department of the University of Cambridge.

We share the University's mission to contribute to society through the pursuit of education, learning and research at the highest international levels of excellence.

www.cambridge.org
Information on this title: www.cambridge.org/9781108969802

DOI: 10.1017/9781108979801

First published 2023

A catalogue record for this publication is available from the British Library.

ISBN 978-1-108-96980-2 Paperback
ISSN 2633-5069 (online)
ISSN 2633-5050 (print)

Metalinguistic Awareness in Second Language Reading Development

Elements in Applied Linguistics

DOI: 10.1017/9781108979801
First published online: February 2023

Sihui Echo Ke
University of Kentucky

Dongbo Zhang
University of Exeter

Keiko Koda
Carnegie Mellon University

Author for correspondence: Sihui Echo Ke, sihui.ke@uky.edu

Abstract: This Element aims to address the complexity of metalinguistic awareness to achieve a thorough account of its impacts on second language (L2) reading development and promote an in-depth understanding of the factors regulating the influence of first language (L1) metalinguistic awareness on L2 reading. It is guided by four questions: 1) To what extent do L1 phonological, orthographic, and morphological awareness correlate with L2 phonological, orthographic, and morphological awareness in L2 readers? 2) To what extent do phonological, orthographic, and morphological awareness correlate with word decoding intralingually in L2 readers? 3) To what extent do L1 phonological, orthographic, and morphological awareness correlate with L2 word decoding in L2 readers? 4) To what extent do the relations in Questions 1–3 vary as a function of linguistic-, learner-, measurement-, and instruction-related factors? This Element is the first to systematically investigate the roles of distinct facets of metalinguistic awareness in L2 reading.

Keywords: metalinguistic awareness, second language reading, phonology, orthography, morphology

ISBNs: 9781108969802 (PB), 9781108979801 (OC)
ISSNs: 2633-5069 (online), 2633-5050 (print)

Contents

1 What Are the Key Concepts?

1.1 What Is Metalinguistic Awareness?

While it is generally agreed that metalinguistic awareness plays a critical role in language acquisition and development, the definition of metalinguistic awareness varies when researchers examine the link between metalinguistic awareness and *X*. Both cognitive and developmental scientists who study child first language (L1) development (e.g., Gombert, 1992; Tunmer et al., 1984) and applied linguists who study second language (L2) teaching and learning have referred to metalinguistic awareness as *explicit or conscious knowledge about language* (see a review in Roehr-Brackin, 2018). Researchers who are interested in the cognitive advantages of bilingualism/multilingualism over monolingualism have proposed that metalinguistic awareness involves two components – *the analytical ability to reflect upon and manipulate formal properties of language* and *the attentional control of the mental mechanism that operates language processing* (Bialystok, 2001; Bialystok & Ryan, 1985). Among researchers of L1 or L2 reading, metalinguistic awareness has been defined as "the ability to reflect on and manipulate the structural features of language" (Nagy, 2007, p. 53; Nagy & Anderson, 1995, p. 2; see also Kuo & Anderson, 2008). Learning to read is fundamentally metalinguistic because learners need to understand how the internal elements of a spoken word relate to units of graphic symbols. Reading in an L2, as compared to reading in an L1, can be even more metalinguistically demanding. Whereas successful adult L2 readers can be well cognizant of sharable metalinguistic resources between two languages and readily apply those resources to facilitate their L2 reading, this process can be a challenging task for children who are learning to read for the first time in an L2.

Metalinguistic awareness, in the context of reading acquisition, is often conceived of as a complex multidimensional and multifaceted construct, involving several related yet distinct components, ranging from segmental understanding (i.e., understanding that words can be segmented into smaller, functionally identifiable units), to structural sensitivity (i.e., the ability to isolate, blend, and combine segmental word information), to functional awareness (i.e., to apply structural understandings for functional purposes such as lexical inferencing)[1] (Ke et al., 2021; Koda & Miller, 2018; Zhang & Koda, 2013).

---

[1] *Lexical inferencing* is defined as "making informed guesses of the meaning of a word in light of all available linguistic cues in combination with the learners' general knowledge of the world, [his/her] awareness of the co-text and [his/her] relevant linguistic knowledge" (Haastrup, 1991, p. 11). It has also been termed as *word learning*, *vocabulary learning*, *word meaning inferencing*, or *semantic gap filling* in the applied linguistics or reading literature.

Researchers have primarily examined three major facets of metalinguistic awareness: phonological awareness (the ability to reflect upon and manipulate phonological units in a language), orthographic awareness (the ability to form, store, and access orthographic representations of words), and morphological awareness (the ability to reflect on and manipulate the morphemic structures of words). Reading has been theorized as an interactive process of phonology, orthography, and morphology (Plaut et al., 1996; Seidenberg & McClelland, 1989). According to Perfetti (2003), the universal process of learning to read involves learning how one's writing system encodes one's spoken language at various levels, with phonology and morphology at the higher mapping level and inclusive of different languages, and orthography at the lower mapping level entailing more language-specific constraints. In regard to the relationship between metalinguistic awareness and L2 reading development, prior studies have been guided by various reading theories (e.g., the Psycholinguistic Grain Size Theory, Ziegler & Goswami, 2005; the Repertoire Theory of Literacy Development, Apel et al., 2004; Masterson & Apel, 2000; the Structural Sensitivity Theory, Kuo & Anderson, 2010; Universal Grammar of Reading, Perfetti, 2003) and models/frameworks of transfer (e.g., the Transfer Facilitation Model, Koda, 2005, 2008; An Interactive Framework of Bilingual Reading Development, Chung et al., 2019) (see Appendix S2 online: osf.io/4z6mw, which includes the coding of thirteen different frameworks/hypotheses/models/theories cited in the selected studies).

This Element is mainly guided by the Lexical Quality Hypothesis (Perfetti, 2007; Perfetti & Hart, 2002), the Repertoire Theory of Literacy Development (Apel et al., 2004; Masterson & Apel, 2000), and the Transfer Facilitation Model (Koda, 2005, 2008). According to the Lexical Quality Hypothesis (Perfetti, 2007; Perfetti & Hart, 2002), successful reading comprehension depends on high-quality lexical knowledge represented by orthography, phonology, morphosyntax, meaning, and the binding of these four features. While the Lexical Quality Hypothesis pertains to the causal relationship between lexical knowledge and reading comprehension and specifies the feature properties such as orthography, phonology, and morphosyntax, it does not directly address how metalinguistic awareness contributes to lexical knowledge or reading ability at the lexical level. In comparison, the Repertoire Theory of Literacy Development (Apel et al., 2004; Masterson & Apel, 2000) proposes explicitly that the development of word spelling and reading ability is subject to the application of phonological, orthographic, and morphological awareness, and provides specific guidance for reading instruction. In other words, teachers should not single out any facet of metalinguistic awareness, but rather concurrently promote different facets of metalinguistic awareness. Last but not least, the Transfer Facilitation Model (Koda, 2005, 2008) provides important insights into cross-language transfer in L2 reading by treating metalinguistic awareness as a window of investigation, whereas other theories cited in previous research either were developed for L1 reading purposes only or examined a wide range of transferable reading subskills instead of focusing on metalinguistic awareness.

1.2 Reciprocal Development of Metalinguistic Awareness, Linguistic Knowledge, and Reading Competence

In this Element, we focus on the contributions from metalinguistic awareness to reading-related outcomes (e.g., word decoding, vocabulary knowledge, and reading comprehension) in L2 reading development. It is important, however, to acknowledge that metalinguistic awareness, reading competence (e.g., reading comprehension), and linguistic knowledge (e.g., vocabulary knowledge) (Koda, 2005; Nagy, 2007; Wagner & Meros, 2010)[2] are developmentally and reciprocally related. Nagy (2007) proposed that metalinguistic awareness is the causal mediator between vocabulary knowledge and reading comprehension (see also Zhang & Koda, 2018). To understand the mechanism underlying this *metalinguistic hypothesis*, four questions need to be answered: 1) How does metalinguistic awareness support reading comprehension? 2) How does vocabulary knowledge support reading comprehension? 3) How does metalinguistic awareness support vocabulary knowledge? and 4) What are the shared and unique contributions of different facets of metalinguistic awareness to reading development?

How does metalinguistic awareness support reading comprehension? Metalinguistic awareness plays at least two important roles in reading development. At the early stage, metalinguistic awareness enables learners to map the elements of spoken language onto the writing system and is thus fundamentally important for word decoding. Later, when learners develop more refined metalinguistic awareness, including deeper understandings of word-internal phonological, orthographic, and morphological structures, they can apply analytical approaches toward lexical inferencing during reading (Koda, 2005; Nagy et al., 2014). These two distinct yet related roles of metalinguistic awareness in reading development are supported by ample empirical evidence that uncovered indirect contributions of various facets of metalinguistic awareness to L1 or L2 reading comprehension via the mediation of word decoding (e.g., L1 Chinese: Li & Wu, 2015; Zhao et al., 2019; L1 English:

---

[2] Bialystok (2001) viewed metalinguistic ability and linguistic knowledge as two distinct constructs. She posited that metalinguistic ability should be measured at the abstract level without being instantiated in any particular language, whereas linguistic knowledge involves knowledge about a particular language.

Badian, 2001; Deacon et al., 2014; just to name a few)[3] or vocabulary knowledge (e.g., L2 Chinese: Ke & Koda, 2019; Leong et al., 2011; L2 English: Kieffer et al., 2013; Nassaji & Geva, 1999; Zhang & Koda, 2012; Zhang & Lin, 2021). Metalinguistic awareness has also been found to contribute directly to reading comprehension. For example, refined morphological awareness in English involves learners' sensitivity to the distributional properties of derived words, which account for a large proportion of words covered in academic English texts (Nagy & Townsend, 2012). This metalinguistic insight helps learners to use the syntactic cues provided by affixes and conduct sentence parsing in word-to-text integration (Levesque et al., 2021; Nagy, 2007; Perfetti & Stafura, 2014). Another rationale that supports the direct contribution of metalinguistic awareness to reading comprehension is that metalinguistic awareness is a subset of metacognition, and metacognition is important for reading comprehension (Nagy, 2007), perhaps more so for L2 learners (Bialystok & Ryan, 1985). According to Gombert (1992), metacognition refers to one's awareness and reflections about one's knowledge, experiences, and learning in general; metalinguistic awareness pertains to the reflections about one's *language* use and learning. In previous interventional studies of readers who have a heightened understanding of their own processes for acquiring knowledge (i.e., metacognition) and who are able to consider how and why language is used (i.e., metalinguistic awareness), findings have demonstrated that the introduction of explicit metacognitive and metalinguistic strategy instruction can positively influence reading comprehension (Williams & Atkins, 2009; Yuill, 2007; Zipke et al., 2009). The logic is that the language in written texts is more decontextualized than the language in spoken conversations; as a result, learners need to pay close attention to and analyze the language in written texts, reflect on the analyzed language, and control these cognitive processes during text reading.

How does vocabulary knowledge support reading comprehension? Vocabulary knowledge is often conceptualized to entail vocabulary size/breadth (how many words a learner knows; Nation, 2001) and vocabulary depth (how well a learner knows the words; Meara, 1996; Read, 1993, 2000). Both dimensions of vocabulary knowledge directly impact reading comprehension. Previous research indicates a very high vocabulary coverage rate for successful reading comprehension, ranging between 95 percent (Liu & Nation, 1985) and 98 percent (Hu & Nation, 2000; Nation, 2006; Schmitt et al., 2011). This clearly underscores the importance

---

[3] The citations here include previous research of two typologically distant writing systems: morphophonemic English and morphosyllabic Chinese. Instead of providing an exhaustive list of references, we have included recent empirical reading studies on English or Chinese either as the L1 or L2.

of vocabulary size in reading comprehension. Independent of the effect of vocabulary size, vocabulary depth makes an additional contribution to explaining variation in reading comprehension (e.g., Qian, 1998; Zhang & Yang, 2016). The direct effect of vocabulary knowledge on reading comprehension has also been supported by a meta-analysis of thirty-seven primary studies on the effects of vocabulary instruction in preK–12th graders whose L1 was English (Elleman et al., 2009). Elleman and colleagues (2009) identified significant, albeit small, improvement in vocabulary and reading comprehension outcomes as a result of vocabulary instruction. In addition, both vocabulary breadth and depth can indirectly contribute to reading comprehension via lexical inferencing while reading (Koda, 2005; Nassaji, 2003, 2006; Paribakht & Wesche, 1999; Qian, 2005). Successful lexical inferencing, either intentional or unintentional, will subsequently fill the semantic gaps of a learner's text representation and predict reading comprehension (Hatakeyama, 2012; Koda & Miller, 2018).

How does metalinguistic awareness support vocabulary knowledge? Metalinguistic awareness and vocabulary knowledge can serve as a bootstrapper for each other. For instance, McBride-Chang and colleagues (2008) tracked the developmental relationships between morphological awareness and vocabulary knowledge in preschoolers in three languages (Cantonese, Mandarin, and Korean) at two time points, and observed bidirectional bootstrapping effects: At Time 1 where vocabulary knowledge, phonological processing, and reasoning skills were controlled, morphological awareness predicted Time 2 vocabulary knowledge across languages; vocabulary knowledge also predicted subsequent morphological awareness, with Time 1 morphological awareness controlled. As reviewed earlier, morphological awareness and vocabulary knowledge are linked via lexical inferencing during reading comprehension. In other words, the ability to productively combine morphemes is viewed as an important skill in inferring meanings of new words (Wagner & Meros, 2010). Furthermore, vocabulary-depth knowledge acquired through formal instruction, such as knowledge of word roots, prefixes, and suffixes, serves as the foundation of morphological awareness (e.g., Zhang & Koda, 2018). One may doubt how the various facets of metalinguistic awareness jointly support vocabulary knowledge development. Regarding oral vocabulary knowledge acquisition, logic would suggest that both phonological and morphological awareness matter because learners need to associate spoken (phonological) forms of words with their meanings (morphemes) (e.g., McBride-Chang et al., 2005). Notably, orthographic awareness also plays a facilitative role in oral vocabulary knowledge acquisition in alphabetic and nonalphabetic languages as orthography has been found to boost learners' recall of novel new words verbally over no orthography in previous quasi-experimental studies (e.g., Chinese in Zhang et al., 2020; English in Ricketts et al., 2009). One possible mechanism through which orthographic awareness supports oral vocabulary knowledge development can be explained by the Lexical Quality Hypothesis (Perfetti, 2007; Perfetti & Hart, 2002). Lexical representation that includes phonology, orthography, and semantics is considered of higher quality than a lexical representation that includes only phonological and semantic information (see also Salins et al., 2022). Regarding print vocabulary knowledge learning, according to Apel and colleagues (2004), phonological, orthographic, and morphological awareness are integral language components in print vocabulary acquisition measured by spelling. Apel and colleagues' position is also consistent with stage-based theories that view reading ability as developing from a *pre-alphabetic* phase to *semiphonetic, phonetic, within-word, syllable conjuncture,* and *derivational constancy* phases (Ehri, 2005; Templeton & Morris, 2000). Last but not least, as Nagy (2007) pointed out, many existing vocabulary knowledge measures are metalinguistic in nature (e.g., word definition skills, Kang, 2013; Ordóñez et al., 2002). Therefore, it is not surprising to find a strong association between metalinguistic awareness and vocabulary knowledge.

What are the shared and unique contributions of different facets of metalinguistic awareness to reading development? Phonological, orthographic, and morphological awareness are three interconnected yet distinct facets of metalinguistic awareness. In a recent structural equation modeling study, Tighe and colleagues (2019) explored a five-factor model of reading comprehension in struggling adult English readers and the interrelationships among these factors (i.e., phonological awareness, orthographic awareness, morphological awareness, word decoding, and vocabulary knowledge). Tighe and colleagues found that, as separate constructs, none of the metalinguistic skills emerged as uniquely predictive of reading comprehension; yet when the three facets of metalinguistic awareness were loaded to a second-order factor, the second-order factor was found to affect reading comprehension indirectly via word decoding and vocabulary knowledge. Although Tighe and colleagues' study focused on struggling adult readers instead of child L2 readers, it was among the first to provide empirical evidence supporting readers' dissociable use of the various facets of metalinguistic awareness for reading comprehension purposes. On the other hand, prior research of English reading comprehension in child and adult readers with or without reading disabilities has identified the unique contribution of morphological awareness to reading comprehension over and above phonological and orthographic awareness (e.g., Apel et al., 2012; Nagy et al., 2003; Tighe et al., 2019). Similar results have been reported in reading in L2 English (e.g., Bae & Joshi, 2018) or a nonalphabetic L1 (e.g., Chinese in Zhang, 2017a). As Kirby and Bowers (2017) put it, morphology is the binding agent of phonological, orthographic, and semantic features of words. There are a few exceptions in L2 reading literature though, suggesting that, out of the three facets of metalinguistic awareness, either phonological awareness or orthographic awareness was among the most important predictors when word decoding instead of reading comprehension was treated as the target reading outcome (e.g., Zhang, 2017b; Zhou et al., 2018). For example, Zhou and colleagues observed that, for Southeast Asian immigrant children learning both English and Chinese as additional languages in Hong Kong primary schools, phonological awareness was the most important factor for word decoding in English, whereas ortho-graphic and morphological awareness were both unique factors of word decoding in Chinese.

In sum, there are multiple direct and indirect paths that connect metalin-guistic awareness, reading comprehension, and vocabulary knowledge together. A notable skill that helps to establish the reciprocal relationships between these three competencies (i.e., covarying with metalinguistic aware-ness, reading comprehension, and vocabulary knowledge) is *lexical inferen-cing* (see Koda, 2005; Nagy et al., 2014). In addition, previous research has also found word decoding to modulate the indirect contribution of metalin-guistic awareness to reading comprehension (e.g., Badian, 2001; Deacon et al., 2014; Li & Wu, 2015; Zhang et al., 2020; Zhao et al., 2019). Last but not least, phonological, orthographic, and morphological awareness are the three most-researched facets of metalinguistic awareness in the literature, and they have been found to make both shared and unique contributions to reading development. Therefore, in the scoping review in Section 3, we aim to explore how and to what extent the various facets of metalinguistic awareness are related to word decoding, lexical inferencing, vocabulary knowledge, and reading comprehension, respectively, in prior L2 reading studies. The meta-analysis reported in Section 4, however, only covers the cross-language relationships between metalinguistic awareness and word decoding. Subskills of L2 reading such as lexical inferencing, vocabulary knowledge, and reading comprehension are not included in the meta-analysis. This is because, according to the scoping review results, prior studies that have measured phonological, orthographic, and morphological awareness simultaneously have focused on child L2 readers instead of adult L2 readers. In addition, word decoding was the most studied outcome; vocabulary knowledge and reading comprehension received far less atten-tion; and little child L2 reading research examined lexical inferencing as a reading-related outcome.

1.3 Transfer Facilitation Effects of Metalinguistic Awareness Across Languages

In this Element, transfer is defined as "automatic activation of well-established first language competencies triggered by second language input" (Koda, 2008, p. 78). Facilitation is the bootstrapping consequence of applying available L1 resources, such as metalinguistic awareness, to L2 reading tasks (Genesee et al., 2006; Koda, 2005, 2008; Riches & Genesee, 2006). Various frameworks have been proposed to inform the understanding of transfer in applied linguistics research in general and in L2 reading research in particular. Examples include:

1. The Contrastive and Typological Framework (Lado, 1957), which views transfer as interference in the L2 due to L1 structural properties;
2. The Linguistic Interdependence Hypothesis, which distinguishes between cognitively and conceptually more and less demanding knowledge, and predicts the conditions under which the learner can demonstrate transfer of knowledge crosslinguistically (Cummins, 1979, 1981);
3. The Common Underlying Cognitive Processes Framework, which states that individual differences in L1 and L2 reading skills can be predicted by a common set of underlying cognitive constructs (such as phonological awareness and decoding; e.g., Geva & Ryan, 1993);
4. The Structural Sensitivity Theory (Kuo & Anderson, 2010), which postulates that "having access to two languages renders structural similarities and differences between languages more salient, thus allowing bilingual children to form representations of language structure at a more abstract level" (p. 365);
5. The Transfer Facilitation Model (Koda, 2005, 2008), which was briefly noted earlier.

Notably, Koda's Transfer Facilitation Model is "the most elaborate theory of transfer to date" (Chung et al., 2019, p. 158). The model specifies that subskills are transferred in L2 reading acquisition rather than a set of L1 linguistic rules or a holistic construct (like L1 reading ability or L1 proficiency). More importantly, metalinguistic awareness is postulated as an important reading subskill that provides a window for crosslinguistic examinations. The Transfer Facilitation Model also highlights the nonvolitional and automatic nature of transfer, and provides predictions on multiple factors that affect transfer of subskills in L2 reading and the conditions for the transfer, including, for example, the joint influence of L1 metalinguistic awareness sophistication and L2 print input experience, as well as L1–L2 distance, which are in line with the following hypotheses on L2 reading.

1. The Script Dependent Hypothesis (SDH) (Geva & Siegel, 2000) suggests that the development of reading component skills is a direct function of orthography transparency; thus, L2 reading efficiency is a direct function of L1 orthography.
2. The Linguistic Coding Differences/Deficit Hypothesis (LCDH) (Sparks et al., 1989, Sparks & Ganschow, 1991) indicates that students who do poorly in a foreign language may have language problems in their L1 that interfere with their ability to learn.
3. The Linguistic Threshold Hypothesis (Alderson, 1984) proposes that a threshold level of L2 linguistic knowledge/proficiency is required for L1 reading skills to transfer to L2.
4. The Short-Circuit Hypothesis (Clarke, 1980) proposes that L2 linguistic knowledge plays a more important role in predicting L2 reading ability development than does L1 reading ability (see also Bernhardt & Kamil, 1995; Carrell, 1991).

None of the four hypotheses mentioned above, however, attempts to specifically explain the transfer of metalinguistic awareness. Accordingly, no predictions have been made in them regarding to what extent L1 metalinguistic awareness transfers and facilitates L2 reading subskill development and under what conditions transfer facilitation occurs. In contrast, Koda (2008) provided four pertinent contentions:

1. Shared metalinguistic awareness (e.g., phonological awareness), once developed in one language, is readily available in the early stage of learning to read in another.
2. Language-specific metalinguistic awareness (e.g., orthographic and morphological awareness) reflects the specific ways in which language elements are graphically encoded in the writing system. When transferred, language-specific metalinguistic awareness, closely attuned to L1 properties, promotes the development of corresponding metalinguistic awareness and reading subskills in L2.
3. When transferred, L1 metalinguistic awareness competencies, reflecting L1 properties, are adjusted through print experience in L2. The degree of adjustment as well as the amount of L2 print experience are influenced by L1–L2 distance (i.e., how closely related L1 and L2 are).
4. The resulting L2 metalinguistic awareness and L2 reading subskills vary systematically in learners with diverse L1 backgrounds.

Since the Transfer Facilitation Model was first proposed by Koda (2005), it has been widely tested in empirical studies (for reviews, see Koda & Ke, 2018;

Koda & Reddy, 2008). The central tenet of the model, which underscores a facilitative transfer effect of L1 metalinguistic awareness, is consistent with the broad conceptualizations of L1 providing resources for L2 reading (Genesee et al., 2006). In addition, the association between L1 and L2 metalinguistic awareness as predicted by the model has been supported by substantial empirical studies on child or adult L2 readers across different linguistic and educational settings (e.g., American university learners of Chinese as a foreign language, Ke & Koda, 2017; American university learners of Chinese as a heritage language, Zhang & Koda, 2021; Chinese heritage children in the United States, Koda et al., 2014; college-level Chinese students who learned English in the United States, Li & Koda, 2022; Chinese children reading English as a foreign language in mainland China, Zhang & Koda, 2013; Japanese university learners of English as a foreign language, Koda & Miller, 2018; Kanada-speaking children learning to read English in India, Reddy & Koda, 2013; and multilingual children in Singapore, Zhang, 2016; Zhang & Ke, 2019), as well as a small number of meta-analytic studies (e.g., Jeon & Yamashita, 2014; Ke et al., 2021; Melby-Lervåg & Lervåg, 2011). Consequently, we have adopted this model to guide our reviews and meta-analysis in the rest of this Element.

In what follows, we first review the findings of five previous meta-analytic studies that are related to (but nonetheless distinct from) our meta-analysis (Section 2). We then provide a scoping review of empirical studies on metalinguistic awareness and L2 reading (Section 3). In Section 4, we present our meta-analysis of intralingual and interlingual correlations of phonological, orthographic, and morphological awareness with word decoding in L2 readers.

2 Evidence from Previous Meta-Analytic and Critical Reviews

2.1 Review Inclusion Criteria

Five meta-analytic studies (i.e., Jeon & Yamashita, 2014; Ke et al., 2021; Melby-Lervåg & Lervåg, 2011; Míguez-Álvarez et al., 2021; Ruan et al., 2018) have been included in the review in this section (as shown in Table 1) because they (1) examined the correlation between at least one facet of metalinguistic awareness (i.e., phonological, orthographic, or morphological awareness) and one reading-related outcome (e.g., word decoding, vocabulary knowledge, or reading comprehension) and (2) either focused on bilingual readers (Jeon & Yamashita, 2014; Ke et al., 2021; Melby-Lervåg & Lervåg, 2011) or both monolingual and bilingual readers (Míguez-Álvarez et al., 2021), or adopted a crosslinguistic perspective comparing correlational relationship(s)

Table 1 Summary of the findings from previous meta-analyses of metalinguistic awareness and reading development.

Meta-analytic study	Correlation (language)	r estimate	Adjusted effect estimate	Effect size[a]	k	Significant moderator(s)	Supplementary note
Cross-language transfer of metalinguistic (phonological and morphological) awareness							
Melby-Lervåg & Lervåg (2011)	L1 PA–L2 PA (mixed)	0.60	0.63	large	16	None was identified despite significant variation in the primary studies.	Age did not have any significant moderating effect.
Ke et al. (2021)	L1 MA–L2 MA (mixed)	0.30	N.A.	small	20	MA measurement type: The effect size was moderate for studies that measured MA with the morphological structure awareness task and minimal for studies that used the Test of Morphological Structure.	
Intralingual relationships between metalinguistic (phonological) awareness and reading in L1							
Ruan et al. (2018)	L1 PA–L1 WD (Chinese)	r1=.30 r2=.26	r1=N.A. r2=.26	small	k1=41 k2=6	None was identified despite significant variation in the primary studies of L1 PA–L1 WD accuracy. There was no significant variation in the primary studies of L1 PA–L1 WD fluency.	WD measurement: r1 was based on WD accuracy; r2 was based on WD fluency.

Table 1 (cont.)

Meta-analytic study	Correlation (language)	r estimate	Adjusted effect estimate	Effect size[a]	k	Significant moderator(s)	Supplementary note
Ruan et al. (2018)	L1 PA–L1 WD (English)	$r1=.55$ $r2=.51$	$r1=.58$ $r2=$N.A.	moderate	$k1=41$ $k2=11$	Grade level and phonological awareness task complexity: For L1 PA–L1 WD fluency, grade level was a significant moderator only for advanced readers. Complex phonological awareness tasks correlated more strongly with the reading outcome.	WD measurement: $r1$ was based on WD accuracy; $r2$ was based on WD fluency.
Míguez-Álvarez et al. (2021)	L1 PA–L1 WD (Spanish)	$r1=.37$ $r2=.29$ $r3=.34$ $r4=.42$ $r5=.34$	N.A.	small to moderate	$k1=39$ $k2=21$ $k3=14$ $k4=9$ $k5=4$	There was a stronger correlation between phonological awareness and nonword reading in bilingual participants compared to monolingual participants.	$r1$ to $r5$ were estimates for the respective relationships of phonemic awareness and word decoding, phonemic awareness and nonword decoding, intrasyllabic awareness and word decoding, syllabic awareness and word decoding, and syllabic

Study	Relationship		Magnitude		k		
Ruan et al. (2018)	L1 PA–L1 RC (Chinese)	0.23	small	0.21	8	Not applicable: No significant variation was found in the primary studies.	awareness and nonword decoding.
Ruan et al. (2018)	L1 PA–L1 RC (English)	0.44	moderate	0.48	20	Phonological awareness task complexity: Complex phonological awareness tasks correlated more strongly with the reading outcome.	
Miguez-Álvarez et al. (2021)	L1 PA–L2 RC (Spanish)	$r1=.40$ $r2=.34$ $r3=.46$	small to moderate	N.A.	$k1=19$ $k2=4$ $k3=6$	None was identified despite significant variation in the primary studies.	$r1$ was based on phonemic awareness; $r2$ was based on intrasyllabic awareness; $r3$ was based on syllabic awareness.
Intralingual relationships between metalinguistic (morphological) awareness and reading in L1							
Ruan et al. (2018)	L1 MA–L1 WD (Chinese)	$r1=.39$ $r2=.39$	small	$r1=N.A.$ $r2=.34$	$k1=41$ $k2=6$	Morphological awareness task: The production tasks correlated more strongly with reading accuracy than the judgment tasks.	WD measurement: $r1$ was based on WD accuracy; $r2$ was based on WD fluency.
Ruan et al. (2018)	L1 MA–L1 WD (English)	$r1=.46$ $r2=.37$	moderate	$r1=48$ $r2=43$	$k1=41$ $k2=11$	Morphological awareness task: The production tasks correlated more strongly with reading accuracy than the judgment tasks.	WD measurement: $r1$ was based on WD accuracy; $r2$ was based on WD fluency.

Table 1 (cont.)

Meta-analytic study	Correlation (language)	r estimate	Adjusted effect estimate	Effect size[a]	k	Significant moderator(s)	Supplementary note
Ruan et al. (2018)	L1 MA–L1 RC (Chinese)	0.36	0.38	small	8	Not applicable: No significant variation was found in the primary studies.	
Ruan et al. (2018)	L1 MA–L1 RC (English)	0.53	0.57	moderate	20	None was identified in spite of significant variation in the primary studies.	

Intralingual relationship between metalinguistic (phonological, orthographic, and morphological) awareness and reading in L2

Ke et al. (2021)	L2 MA–L2 WD (mixed)	0.46	0.50	moderate	34	MA measurement type: The effect size was small for studies that measured MA with the morphological relatedness task, and moderate for studies that used the Test of MorphologicalStructure.	
Jeon & Yamashita (2014)	L2 PA–L2 RC (mixed)	0.48	N.A.	moderate	11	Not applicable: No moderating analysis was conducted despite significant variation in the primary studies.	They used the term "phonological knowledge" instead of "awareness."
Jeon & Yamashita (2014)	L2 OA–L2 RC (mixed)	0.51	0.54	moderate	5	Not applicable: No significant variation was found in the primary studies.	They used the term "orthographic knowledge" instead of "awareness."

| Ke et al. (2021) | L2 MA–L2 RC (mixed) | 0.52 | 0.54 | moderate | 17 | Age: The effect size was bigger for children in the upper elementary grades. |

Transfer facilitation of metalinguistic (phonological and morphological) awareness in L2 reading

Study	Measure					Notes
Melby-Lervåg & Lervåg (2011)	L1 PA–L2 WD (mixed)	0.44	0.39	small	14	None was identified despite significant variation in the primary studies. Age did not have any significant moderating effect.
Ke et al. (2021)	L1 MA–L2 WD (mixed)	0.35	N.A.	small	19	None was identified despite significant variation in the primary studies.
Ke et al. (2021)	L1 MA–L2 RC (mixed)	0.39	0.37	small	6	Not applicable: No significant variation was found in the primary studies.

Notes. L1 = first language; L2 = second language; PA = phonological awareness; OA = orthographic awareness; MA = morphological awareness; WD = word decoding; RC = reading comprehension; N.A. = not applicable. [a] The interpretation of effect sizes (rs) is based on Plonsky and Oswald's (2014) estimates for small, medium, and large correlations (r=.25, .40, .60, respectively).

between two languages (e.g., Chinese and English in Ruan et al., 2018).[4] We tabulated and compared the findings of these five studies. We noted that a few other meta-analyses reported Cohen's *d* (mean differences) rather than correlation coefficient *r*, such as Bratlie and colleagues (2022) and Goodwin and Ahn (2010, 2013). In addition, Chung and colleagues (2019) was a critical descriptive review rather than a meta-analysis. The findings of these meta-analyses and critical review were not directly compared. Nevertheless, we consider them when discussing potential moderators of interest below.

Among the five meta-analyses included in the review below, notably four focused on child bilingual readers and only one involved adult L2 readers in their sample populations (i.e., Jeon & Yamashita, 2014). Jeon and Yamashita was also the only meta-analysis reporting a pertinent correlation between L2 orthographic awareness and an L2 reading outcome (i.e., reading comprehension),[5] whereas all of the other four meta-analyses reported correlations between phonological or morphological awareness and a reading outcome (word decoding or reading comprehension). None of the five meta-analyses examined the relationship between any facet of metalinguistic awareness and vocabulary knowledge or lexical inferencing.

2.2 Evidence Supporting Cross-Language Transfer Facilitation of Metalinguistic Awareness

Table 1 summarizes the findings from previous meta-analyses of metalinguistic awareness and reading development. In the table, we present the findings on correlations between L1 and L2 metalinguistic awareness, intralingual correlations between metalinguistic awareness and reading outcomes, as well as interlingual correlations of L1 metalinguistic awareness with L2 reading outcomes. Our interpretation of effect sizes (*r*s) is based on Plonsky and Oswald's (2014) estimates for small, medium, and large correlations (*r* = .25, .40, .60, respectively).

In regard to the extent to which metalinguistic awareness in L1 and L2 are related, as shown in the upper panel of Table 1, Melby-Lervåg and Lervåg's (2011) meta-analysis of phonological awareness and L2 reading development

---

[4] We noted that Branum-Martin and colleagues (2012) also conducted a meta-analysis of bilingual phonological awareness and analyzed correlational variation in L2 English learners of different L1s. But Míguez-Álvarez and colleagues (2021) and Ruan and colleagues (2018) provided more up-to-date reviews based on larger sample pools.

[5] Jeon and Yamashita (2014) used the term "orthographic knowledge" instead of "orthographic awareness." According to Nagy and colleagues' (2014) review of morphological knowledge and reading development, the terms "knowledge," "awareness," and "processing" have been used interchangeably in the literature. "Knowledge" is the overarching term for "awareness" and "processing."

suggested a large correlation between L1 and L2 phonological awareness ($r = .60$), while Ke and colleagues' (2021) meta-analysis on morphological awareness identified a small correlation between L1 and L2 morphological awareness ($r = .30$). The finding that the two facets of metalinguistic awareness correlated to different extents in two languages (i.e., higher for phonological awareness and lower for morphological awareness) is consistent with Koda and colleagues' (2014) position that phonological awareness is a language-general and shared resource across languages (see also Geva & Ryan, 1993), whereas morphological awareness is a language-specific and shareable resource. To the best of our knowledge, there is no meta-analytic evidence in the literature on cross-language correlations for orthographic awareness. Chung and colleagues' (2019) critical review, however, provided an insight into this issue: L1 and L2 orthographic awareness[6] were significantly correlated between two Roman alphabets (e.g., English–French: Chung et al., 2018; Commissaire et al., 2011; Deacon et al., 2009; Pasquarella et al., 2014; English–Spanish: Sun-Alperin & Wang, 2011); yet few studies supported any significant correlation of orthographic awareness between different L1 and L2 scripts (e.g., Chinese–English: Gottardo et al., 2001; Russian–English: Abu-Rabia, 2001).

As the middle panels of Table 1 illustrate, the relative correlations between L1 phonological awareness and L1 reading-related outcomes (i.e., word decoding and reading comprehension) and those between L1 morphological awareness and L1 reading outcomes varied in previous meta-analyses, subject to the influence of the target language (Chinese and English: Ruan et al., 2018; Spanish: Míguez-Álvarez et al., 2021). The correlations between phonological awareness and reading-related outcomes in L1 Chinese were all small, whereas the magnitudes were moderate in L1 English and ranged from small to moderate in L1 Spanish. In addition, the correlations between morphological awareness and reading-related outcomes in L1 Chinese were higher than those between phonological awareness and reading in L1 Chinese, but still fell within the small range. The correlations between morphological awareness and reading-related outcomes in L1 English, however, were moderate. Regarding intralingual correlations between L2 metalinguistic awareness and L2 reading-related outcomes, regardless of the facet of metalinguistic awareness or reading outcomes under examination, the evidence was consistent across the previous meta-analyses; that is, the correlations were significant and moderate. Taken together, these findings on intralingual correlations demonstrated less variation in the relationship between metalinguistic awareness and reading outcomes in L2 than in L1.

---

[6] Chung and colleagues (2019) used the term "orthographic processing" instead of "orthographic awareness" in their review.

Finally, as shown in the bottom panel of Table 1, interlingually speaking, the findings are consistent across previous meta-analyses – the correlations between L1 metalinguistic (phonological or morphological) awareness and L2 reading-related outcomes (word decoding or reading comprehension) were all small yet significant.

2.3 Evidence Related to Factors Impacting the Transfer Facilitation of Metalinguistic Awareness in L2 Reading

Table 1 also summarizes the (non)significant moderating effects. One of the theory-driven factors is L1–L2 distance, which was, for example, operationalized as L1–L2 writing system type in Ke and colleagues (2021) and Melby-Lervåg and Lervåg (2021) (see also Section 1.3). No significant moderating effect, however, was identified for this factor. This finding suggests that, regardless of L1–L2 distance, L1 metalinguistic awareness not only transfers at the construct level (i.e., significant correlations between corresponding L1 and L2 metalinguistic awareness), but also has crossover facilitation effects on L2 reading-related outcomes (i.e., significant correlations of L1 metalinguistic awareness with L2 reading abilities).

Proficiency in L2 is another theory-driven factor related to L2 print input experience (Chung et al., 2019; Koda, 2005, 2007, 2008) that may impact transfer of metalinguistic awareness (see relevant discussion in Section 1.3). Nevertheless, it was not examined in the selected meta-analyses. Although Jeon and Yamashita (2014) did consider the influence of L2 proficiency on the relationship between L1 and L2 reading comprehension, they did not conduct any moderator analysis investigating its impact on the relationship between metalinguistic awareness and reading in L2. Pertinent and indirect evidence of the influence of L2 proficiency may be found in the recent meta-analysis by Bratlie and colleagues (2022). Bratlie and colleagues compared morphological knowledge between language minority and language majority children, and found that there were moderate to large differences between the two groups. As part of their moderator analysis, the authors found that some continuous variables such as vocabulary, syntactic knowledge, and reading comprehension significantly predicted the group difference. In addition, Bratlie and colleagues did not find any significant differences in morphological knowledge between Chinese L1 children acquiring English, Spanish L1 children acquiring English, and Turkish L1 children acquiring Dutch. The significant gap in language minority children's morphological knowledge in the societal language or L2 might be attributed to their relatively low proficiency in that language because, as discussed in Section 1.3, a threshold of L2 linguistic knowledge or proficiency may need to be passed for language minority children to benefit from their L1 reading subskills such as metalinguistic awareness.

In addition to theory-driven factors, construct-, learner-, measurement-, and instruction-related factors must also be considered (Chung et al., 2019; Gottardo et al., 2021; Ke et al., 2021). At the construct level, metalinguistic awareness consists of three major components – phonological, orthographic, and morphological awareness – each being a multidimensional/multifaceted construct itself. Phonological awareness can be further categorized into phonemic awareness, intrasyllabic awareness, and syllabic awareness based on different linguistic grain sizes (Branum-Martin et al., 2012; Míguez-Álvarez et al., 2021; Ziegler & Goswami, 2005, 2006). In a meta-analysis of Spanish phonological awareness in Spanish monolinguals and bilinguals whose L1 is mainly English, Míguez-Álvarez and colleagues (2021) observed the largest correlation for syllabic awareness. In comparison, in a meta-analysis of bilingual readers of mixed language backgrounds, Branum-Martin and colleagues (2012) identified greater cross-language correlations in phonological awareness tasks that measured multiple grain sizes than those that measured syllabic awareness alone. Branum-Martin and colleagues speculated that phonological awareness manipulating multiple grain sizes may involve processes that are more highly related across languages.

The findings about cross-language transfer of orthographic awareness are inclusive. Evidence that supports the shareability of orthographic awareness in two languages was mainly based on lexical orthographic processing in two alphabetic scripts (see a review by Chung et al., 2019). However, in primary studies of both sublexical and lexical orthographic awareness in two typologically different scripts (e.g., Chinese and English in Wang et al., 2009, 2014), there was no significant positive correlation or the correlation was even negative between L1 and L2 orthographic awareness.

Lastly, for the conceptualization of morphological awareness, there have been two different approaches. One approach adopts a continuum view of morphological awareness as more language independent or more language specific. A language-independent facet of morphology involves segmentation of words into sublexical components (referred to as a basic facet by Zhang & Koda, 2013 or structural awareness by Zhang & Koda, 2018), whereas a language-specific facet involves mapping morphological information onto graphic symbols (referred to as a "refined facet" by Zhang & Koda, 2013 or "functional awareness" by Zhang & Koda, 2018). The other approach is based on word formation rules and categorizes morphological awareness into inflectional, derivational, and compound awareness (e.g., Bratlie et al., 2022). In a meta-analysis that compared morphological knowledge in language minority and language majority children (mainly readers of English), Bratlie and colleagues observed larger variances in primary studies that measured inflectional awareness than in those that measured derivational or compounding awareness. However, Ke and colleagues' (2021) meta-analysis of morphological awareness in bilingual child readers did not identify any significant moderating effect of word formation rules.

At the learner level, an often-examined factor was age/grade level. Previous meta-analyses either operationalized factors of this type as lower versus upper grade level in subgroup analyses (Goodwin & Ahn, 2013; Ke et al., 2021; Melby-Lervåg & Lervåg, 2011) or treated age as a continuous variable in meta-regression analyses (e.g., Branum-Martin et al., 2012). No significant age effect was found for the transfer of phonological awareness between L1 and L2 (e.g., Branum-Martin et al., 2012; Melby-Lervåg & Lervåg, 2011). However, significant moderating effects of age/grade level were found in meta-analyses of morphological awareness. For example, Goodwin and Ahn's (2013) meta-analysis investigated the effects of English morphological intervention in readers of mixed backgrounds (e.g., English-only learners, English language learners, and children with learning disabilities), and found that morphological intervention led to significant improvement in morphological knowledge and reading-related outcomes in a broad range of grade levels from kindergarten to middle school levels. Furthermore, Ke and colleagues (2021) identified a bigger correlation between L2 morphological awareness and L2 reading comprehension in children at the upper elementary grades than children between kindergarten and grade two.

Regarding measurement-related factors, it is generally agreed in the literature that how metalinguistic awareness and reading-related outcomes are measured contributes significantly to the variation in primary studies. Recent studies found that 1) complex phonological awareness tasks correlated more strongly with different reading-related outcomes (Ruan et al., 2018); 2) phonological awareness correlated more strongly with nonword reading than with real word reading in bilingual readers (Míguez-Álvarez et al., 2021); and 3) a larger variation existed in studies examining phonological awareness and word reading accuracy than those on phonological awareness and word reading fluency (Ruan et al., 2018). For morphological awareness, larger correlations were observed for studies that measured oral and expressive/productive morphological awareness than those measuring written and receptive/judgmental morphological awareness (Bratlie et al., 2022; Ruan et al., 2018). Ke and colleagues (2021) identified eight specific types of morphological awareness measured in the literature and found a larger correlation for studies that used the morphological structure task (e.g., McBride-Chang et al., 2005) than those using the Test of Morphological Structure (Carlisle, 2000). For orthographic awareness, due to the small number of primary studies, moderator analysis has barely been conducted in previous meta-analyses. Georgiou and colleagues' (2021) meta-analysis on dyslexic and typical readers (mostly English readers) found no moderating effect of orthographic awareness measurement (i.e., accuracy vs. response time measures). No meta-analysis, however, has been conducted in L2 readers where any moderating measurement effect was tested for orthographic awareness.

Finally, instruction-related factors (e.g., medium of instruction) seems to have been underexamined in previous meta-analyses (except Melby-Lervåg & Lervåg, 2011). Melby-Lervåg and Lervåg did not find any significant effect of medium of instruction on the relationship between L1 phonological awareness and L2 word decoding. The overall lack of attention to instruction-related factors could be partially due to the confounding effects of simultaneously examining multiple factors, either intentionally or unintentionally (Gottardo et al., 2021). For example, L2 as the medium of instruction can be applied to different societal settings (e.g., L2 as the societal language in English-as-a-second-language/ESL classrooms with learners of lower socioeconomic status; or L2 as the non-societal language in dual-language immersion programs with learners of higher socioeconomic status).

To sum up, previous meta-analytic reviews of metalinguistic awareness and reading development have mainly focused on phonological and morphological awareness and their within- and cross-language contributions to reading in child bilingual readers. Much less attention has been paid to adult L2 readers. Reading-related outcomes have largely focused on word decoding. There has been little attention to the correlations of metalinguistic awareness with vocabulary knowledge, lexical inferencing, or reading comprehension. Also, while the evidence seems to converge on the shareability of phonological and morphological awareness between two languages, the shareability of orthographic awareness has not been systematically examined. Overall, it remains unclear the extent to which different facets of metalinguistic awareness correlate with different reading-related outcomes intralingually and interlingually. Lastly, inconclusive evidence can be drawn regarding significant factors moderating the within- and cross-language correlations between metalinguistic awareness and L2 reading.

3 A Scoping Review of Empirical Research between 2009 and 2021

3.1 Literature Search, Inclusion and Exclusion Criteria, and Coding

Literature Search. We conducted a three-step literature search (see Figure 1). First, our search prioritized research exploring orthographic awareness in L2 reading because orthographic awareness has received much less attention than phonological or morphological awareness in previous meta-analyses and other

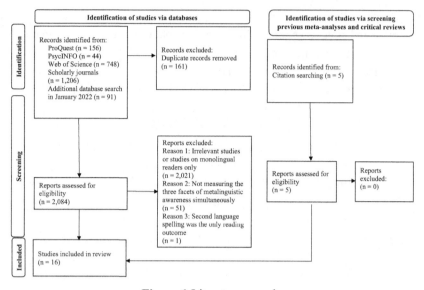

Figure 1 Literature search.

reviews, as indicated in Section 2. Two sets of keywords, including "ortho-graphic knowledge" OR "orthographic awareness" OR "orthographic process-ing" OR "orthographic skill" OR "ortho-" AND "second language" OR "L2" OR "bilingual" OR "L3" OR "third language" OR "multilingual" OR "add-itional language" were used in Boolean searches in three electronic databases: ProQuest (including three subdatabases, namely, ERIC, LLBA, and ProQuest Dissertations and Global Theses), PsycINFO, and Web of Science. The data-base search was first conducted in December 2021 with another search in January 2022. Second, we examined the references of twenty-four meta-analytic and critical reviews of phonological awareness, orthographic aware-ness, or morphological awareness (see the list in Appendix A), looking for studies that *simultaneously* measured phonological, orthographic, and morpho-logical awareness in L2 readers. Third, manual searches were conducted among six scholarly journals: *Applied Psycholinguistics*; *Journal of Research in Reading*; *Language Learning*; *Reading and Writing*; *Reading Research Quarterly*, and *Scientific Studies of Reading*. As of January 31, 2022, a total of 2,245 studies, including duplicated reports, were identified. After screening using a priori criteria described below, sixteen studies ($N = 2,654$) with nineteen independent samples were included for subsequent analysis. The complete list of the included studies can be found in Appendix B. From these search results, the first research trend we noticed is that the number of L2 reading studies simultaneously measuring all three facets of metalinguistic awareness is considerably smaller than the number of those examining one or two facets, as revealed in previous meta-analyses. More specifically, forty-seven studies were identified for phonological awareness by Melby-Lervåg and Lervåg's (2011) meta-analysis and thirty-four studies were found for morphological awareness by Ke and colleagues' (2021) meta-analysis.

Inclusion and Exclusion Criteria. Primary studies included for review in this Element met five criteria: 1) they were written in English between 1990 and 2021; 2) they included participants without a learning or reading disability; 3) they presented empirical data based on direct testing of phonological, orthographic, AND morphological awareness either in L1 or L2; 4) they reported data based on direct testing of at least one L2 measure, such as metalinguistic awareness, word decoding, vocabulary knowledge, lexical inferencing, or reading comprehension; and 5) they reported sample size and data for calculating effect sizes, including the correlation coefficient *r* and/or descriptive statistics with means and standard deviations. We excluded duplication reports as well as studies on L1 or monolingual readers only.

Coding. Detailed procedures of coding effect sizes and moderators are reported in Section 4.2. The complete dataset as well as the coding scheme (as shown in Appendix S1) is available online: osf.io/4z6mw. The first author coded the data twice. For effect size data, the intracoder reliability was .98. For categorical variables and qualitative coding, the first author resolved any inconsistencies via a third check.

3.2 An Overview of the Research Methodologies in the Selected Studies

The meta-analysis reported in Section 4 included sixteen correlational studies published between 2009 and 2021 with data collected from nineteen independent samples of child L2 readers ($N = 2,654$) in seven major locations (i.e., Canada, Hong Kong SAR China, Israel, mainland China, Singapore, South Korea, and the United States).[7] None of the studies included adult L2 participants. All studies were of a cross-sectional and observational design, except Luo (2013), which adopted a longitudinal design.

Table 2 illustrates the number of independent study samples and mean correlations (*r*) for the relationships between the various facets of metalinguistic awareness and different reading-related outcomes. These outcomes included word decoding, reading comprehension, and vocabulary knowledge. More specifically, the results indicated that most of the included L2 child reading studies had focused

---

[7] An exception is Luo's (2013) study, which was based on an unpublished doctoral dissertation.

Table 2 Overall mean correlations between metalinguistic awareness and reading subskills in child bilingual readers (*k*=19).

Transfer of metalinguistic awareness between L1 and L2		
Outcome	***k***	**Mean correlation (*r*)**
L1 PA–L2 PA	7	.44
L1 OA–L2 OA	8	.30
L1 MA–L2 MA	8	.28
Within-L2 relationships		
Outcome	***k***	**Mean correlation (*r*)**
L2 PA–L2 WD	11	.40
L2 PA–L2 RC	4	.23
L2 PA–L2 VOC	9	.28
L2 OA–L2 WD	12	.47
L2 OA–L2 RC	4	.46
L2 OA–L2 VOC	10	.31
L2 MA–L2 WD	10	.46
L2 MA–L2 RC	4	.55
L2 MA–L2 VOC	10	.50
Within-L1 relationships		
Outcome	***k***	**Mean correlation (*r*)**
L1 PA–L1 WD	11	.27
L1 PA–L1 RC	1	.33
L1 PA–L1 VOC	4	.20
L1 OA–L1 WD	11	.34
L1 OA–L1 RC	1	N.A.
L1 OA–L1 VOC	4	.08
L1 MA–L1 WD	11	.38
L1 MA–L1 RC	1	N.A.
L1 MA–L1 VOC	4	.41
Transfer facilitation effects		
Outcome	***k***	**Mean correlation (*r*)**
L1 PA–L2 WD	10	.39
L1 PA–L2 RC	1	N.A.
L1 PA–L2 VOC	4	.32
L1 OA–L2 WD	9	.34
L1 OA–L2 RC	3	.05
L1 OA–L2 VOC	1	N.A.
L1 MA–L2 WD	11	.33
L1 MA–L2 RC	3	.22
L1 MA–L2 VOC	6	.28

Notes. L1 = first language; L2 = second language; PA = phonological awareness; OA = orthographic awareness; MA = morphological awareness; WD = word decoding; RC = reading comprehension; VOC = vocabulary knowledge. N.A. = not applicable.

on the associations between metalinguistic awareness and word decoding, followed by the associations between L1 and L2 metalinguistic awareness. Very limited attention has been paid to the relationships between metalinguistic awareness and reading comprehension or vocabulary knowledge. No selected studies examined the effects of metalinguistic awareness on lexical inferencing.

When sample participants' L1 and L2 were both considered, a total of twelve languages (i.e., Arabic, Chinese, English, French, Hebrew, Hindi, Indonesian, Korean, Nepali, Russian, Tagalog, and Urdu) and four writing systems (i.e., abjad, alphabet, alphasyllabary, and morphosyllabary) were represented. Out of the nineteen independent samples, there were seven types of L1–L2 combinations: L1 English–L2 Chinese ($k = 2$); L1 Arabic–L2 English ($k = 1$); L1 Chinese–L2 English ($k = 8$); L1 Korean–L2 English ($k = 3$); L1 Hebrew/Russian–L2 English ($k = 2$); L1 South Asian languages–L2 English ($k = 2$)[8]; and L1 English–L2 French ($k = 1$). Grades ranged from kindergarten through grade eight, with a mean age of 109 months. Eleven study samples included participants of the language majority group, seven included the minority group, and one sample contained mixed groups. Regarding medium of instruction, five samples included school instruction in the target L2.

3.3 Study Quality Evaluation

To evaluate the quality of the selected studies (after Marsden et al., 2018), we have summarized the internal reliabilities (based on Cronbach's alpha) of pertinent measures reported in primary studies in Table 3. All primary studies reported the internal reliability (Cronbach's alpha) for at least one instrument. Orthographic awareness tasks seemed slightly less reliable than phonological and morphological awareness tasks, while word decoding tasks appeared to be more reliable than reading comprehension and vocabulary knowledge tasks. In general, the mean reliability (except L2 word decoding tasks, mean Cronbach's alpha = .93) seemed to be lower than that reported in previous second language acquisition research (the median reliability of second language acquisition research focusing on reading skills was .86 according to Plonsky & Derrick, 2016). According to Plonsky and Derrick, the 25th, 50th, and 75th percentiles of instrument reliability coefficients for second language acquisition research in general were 74, .82, and .89, respectively. Thus, the mean task reliabilities of the selected studies fall between the 25th and 50th percentiles.

---

[8] Authors in the primary studies (i.e., Wong & Zhou, 2021; Zhou et al., 2018) did not name the exact L1s, but reported participants' ethnic backgrounds, including Filipino, Indian, Indonesian, Nepalese, and Pakistani.

Table 3 Instrument reliability information (Cronbach's alpha) reported in the independent samples.

Construct	k	Mean	Min.	Max.
L1 phonological awareness	12	.83	.63	.96
L2 phonological awareness	14	.81	.70	.97
L1 orthographic awareness	11	.73	.32	.95
L2 orthographic awareness	15	.73	.48	.89
L1 morphological awareness	14	.80	.34	.96
L2 morphological awareness	16	.78	.30	.95
L1 word decoding	9	.84	.64	.98
L2 word decoding	14	.93	.73	.99
L1 reading comprehension	1	.75	.75	.75
L2 reading comprehension	4	.81	.78	.84
L1 vocabulary knowledge	4	.83	.78	.91
L2 vocabulary knowledge	8	.83	.59	.97

Notes. L1 = first language; L2 = second language.

In addition, following Hohn and colleagues' (2019) assessment protocols, we coded and evaluated a total of eleven study quality indices. These indices included the adequacy of conclusions made in the primary study; study design; information found in literature reviews such as theoretical frameworks, the measures used, missing data, and attrition rates; power considerations; the publication status of the primary studies; statistical analyses used; sample-size considerations; reliability estimates; and validity concerns. Due to limitations of space, the complete coding is presented in Appendix S2 online: osf.io/4z6mw.

3.4 Definitions and Measures of Metalinguistic Awareness in the Selected Studies

To recapitulate, just as metalinguistic awareness has been defined in different ways in the literature, there have been different definitions and measures of the three major facets of metalinguistic awareness. This section summarizes the various operationalizations for each facet in the selected studies. Since the number and complexity of metalinguistic awareness measures is a potential moderator on the relationship between metalinguistic awareness and L2 reading (see the meta-analytic results in Section 4), the measures reviewed in this section can also provide methodological implications for future research. Complete coding can be found in Appendix S3 online: osf.io/4z6mw.

Definitions and Measures of Phonological Awareness. Only eleven of the nineteen independent study samples provided an explicit definition of phonological awareness. These definitions can be categorized into four major types:

1. The ability to perceive and manipulate sound units of spoken language (Goswami & Bryant, 1990, as cited in Wang et al., 2009).
2. The ability to identify, isolate, or delete phonemes from a word (Russak, 2020).
3. The ability to process phonemes is typically called phonemic awareness, whereas phonological awareness is a general term referring to the ability to manipulate several units of spoken languages, such as syllables or onsets and rimes in addition to phonemes (Bae & Joshi, 2018).
4. The sensitivity to the segmental as well as suprasegmental features of Chinese phonology (Halliday, 1981, as cited in Zhang, 2017b).

The first definition is a generic definition referring to a learner's awareness of the sound structure of a language; the second type is specifically about phonemic awareness; the third definition, more broadly speaking, includes phonemic, intrasyllabic, and syllabic awareness; and the last is language specific and includes a focus on Chinese tone (a suprasegmental feature) awareness. Influenced by the various types of definitions, phonological awareness measures were operationalized at different levels in the selected studies: at the phoneme level only ($k = 6$), at phoneme and intrasyllable levels ($k = 3$), at phoneme and syllable levels ($k = 3$), at intrasyllable and syllable levels ($k = 4$), at intrasyllable and suprasegmental levels ($k = 2$), and at the syllable level only ($k = 1$).

There were four approaches to measuring phonological awareness:

1. Deletion (e.g., "Say 'three' without the sound /r/." See Abu-Rabia & Sanitsky, 2010);
2. Segmentation and counting (e.g., "Identify the number of speech sounds in the word 'cat.'" /k/, /a/, /t/. See Bae & Joshi, 2018);
3. Categorization/odd-one-out (e.g., "Choose which one of the three syllables does not share either the onset, rime, or tone with the other two syllables." See Wang et al., 2009);
4. Tone discrimination (e.g., "Identify the third syllable [/jiàn/] that differs in tone from the other two syllables [/kě/ and /lěng/]." See Zhang, 2017b).

The selected studies commonly asked participants to respond orally or provide answers to multiple-choice questions in paper-and-pencil packets after listening. Notably, the four approaches reviewed above do not represent an exhaustive list of phonological awareness measures in that a number of measures described in previous reviews (e.g., McBride-Chang, 1995; Schatschneider et al., 1999; Stahl & Murray, 1994) were not used in the selected studies, including, for example:

1. (First-) Sound to word matching (e.g., "Does fish begin with /f/?");
2. Blending ("What does /f-i-sh/" say?");
3. Position analysis (e.g., "Say 'nelf.' Now what sound comes after the /l/ in this nonsense word?").

Definitions and Measures of Orthographic Awareness. Apel and colleagues (2019) provided a comprehensive review of orthographic knowledge at two levels (i.e., sublexical and lexical) and emphasized the differences between measuring implicit orthographic knowledge and explicit orthographic awareness. Lexical orthographic knowledge refers to the stored mental representations of known words or word parts; sublexical orthographic knowledge refers to the rules, positions, or patterns for a letter or letter concatenations (in English, for example) (see also Apel, 2011). Implicit orthographic knowledge is captured in a setting where learners are not overtly asked to think about or consider what they know about orthography (e.g., spontaneous spelling). In contrast, explicit orthographic awareness requires learners to actively think about or reflect on their knowledge of orthography. A commonly used lexical orthographic awareness task is orthographic word choice, in which participants are asked to choose the correct spelling of a real word while facing the actual correct spelling of the real word and a pseudoword with an incorrect spelling (e.g., "rain–rane"). An often-cited sublexical orthographic awareness task is an orthographic word-likeness task, in which participants are asked to choose from a pair of pseudowords, one following legal orthographic conventions and the other violating orthographic conventions (e.g., "gool–giil"). In the nineteen independent study samples, eleven provided pertinent definitions of orthographic awareness, and two definitions seemed to be aligned with Apel and colleagues' (2019) conceptualization of orthographic awareness at lexical and sublexical levels, which orthographic processing tasks have traditionally tapped into:

1. Individual word-specific representations or letter patterns that occur across many words (e.g., Deacon et al., 2009);
2. One's knowledge of word spelling regularities and permissible letter sequences in a word (e.g., Zhao et al., 2017).

The coding results indicated that three samples measured both lexical and sublexical orthographic awareness, five samples measured lexical orthographic awareness only, and eleven samples measured sublexical orthographic awareness only.

Again, there were definitions specific to the Chinese language (e.g., students' visual–orthographic sensitivity to Chinese characters and their awareness of the representational functions of the semantic radicals, Wong & Zhou, 2021; or knowledge about Chinese radicals and the sensitivity to their spatial configurations, Zhang, 2017b). In the selected studies on readers of Chinese, sublexical orthographic awareness was captured with tasks consisting of items on strokes, radicals, and individual characters, while lexical orthographic awareness was measured with tasks of two-character words.

Definitions and Measures of Morphological Awareness. Not all study samples provided a clear definition of morphological awareness; only eleven out of nineteen did so, mostly following Carlisle's (1995) general definition of morphological awareness as "conscious awareness of the morphemic structure of words and [the] ability to reflect on and manipulate that structure" (p. 194). A language-specific operational definition was also included in some studies. For instance, in Zhang's (2017a) study, morphological awareness was defined as learners' sensitivity to homography and morphological compounding, which are both prevalent in Chinese.

In previous meta-analytic research (e.g., Ke et al., 2021), eight different morphological awareness measures have been identified: 1) affix choice (after Singson et al., 2000); 2) morphological structure awareness (e.g., McBride-Chang et al., 2005); 3) morphological decomposition (e.g., Saiegh-Haddad & Geva, 2008); 4) morphological relatedness (e.g., Saiegh-Haddad & Geva, 2008); 5) riddle guess (e.g., Berninger & Nagy, 1999); 6) sentence analogy (after Nunes et al., 1997); 7) the Test of Morphological Structure (after Carlisle, 2000), and 8) the Wug Test (e.g., Eviatar et al., 2018). We produced similar findings based on sixteen of the selected studies for the present meta-analysis. In addition, a Chinese-specific measure (i.e., homophone/homograph discrimination) was identified (e.g., in Zhang, 2017b). For that measure, participants were presented with groups of three words of two characters that shared a homograph. For each group, they were asked to identify the word where the meaning of the target character was different from that in the other two words. For example, in both "商业, /shāngyè/, business" and "商品, /shāngpǐn/, product," "商, /shāng/" means "commerce"; however, in "商量, /shāngliáng/, discuss," "商/shāng/" means "discuss" or "consult."

There was great variation in how the selected studies operationalized the construct of morphological awareness. Take word formation rules, for example. Two independent study samples included inflected words only; two included derived words only; eight included compound words only; one included inflected and derived words; two included derived and compound words; one included inflected, derived, and compound words; and three included compound words and homophones/homographs.

The selected studies also varied in the modality/modalities used for measuring morphological awareness. Unlike phonological awareness measures that mainly assessed spoken languages only, morphological awareness measures often involve a combination of spoken and written modalities. This is not surprising because morphological awareness is considered as a binding agent that strengthens the links between the orthographic, phonological, and meaning representation of morphemes and words (Kirby & Bowers, 2017; Nagy et al., 2014). Kuo and Anderson (2008) termed morphological awareness measured in the written modality as "grapho-morphological awareness," namely "the ability to reflect upon how semantic information is encoded in the orthography and how orthography provides cues to meaning" (p. 54) (see also Chen et al., 2021). Other researchers differentiated oral morphological awareness from written morphological awareness and identified them as "preliterate" versus "postliterate" morphological awareness (e.g., Pan et al., 2016). In the nineteen independent study samples, six samples measured morphological awareness using oral modality, two were in the written modality, three were based on mixed modalities, and eight samples did not report the measurement modality.

3.5 Summary

To reiterate, a total of sixteen studies or nineteen independent study samples that considered all three facets of metalinguistic awareness (i.e., phonological, orthographic, and morphological awareness) were selected for the scoping review and subsequent meta-analysis. The sample participants were K–8 bilingual children ($N = 2,654$) of twelve languages and four writing systems when both L1 and L2 were considered. The majority of the samples included English as the target L2. The selected studies were conducted in seven major locations (i.e., Canada, Hong Kong SAR China, Israel, mainland China, Singapore, South Korea, and the United States). Only one study adopted a longitudinal design; the rest were observational and cross-sectional.

The selected L2 reading studies predominantly examined the relationships between metalinguistic awareness and word decoding in L1 and L2. They did not include sufficient evidence for further meta-analysis of other reading-related outcomes, such as vocabulary knowledge, lexical inferencing, and reading comprehension.

We also reviewed the definitions and measures of the three facets of metalinguistic awareness. Only about half (i.e., eleven) of the nineteen independent study samples provided clear construct definitions. Due to the various operational definitions adopted in the selected studies, there was great variation in how researchers measured the three facets of metalinguistic awareness. We also found that, for studies of nonalphabetic languages like Chinese, language-specific definitions and measures were adopted (e.g., Wong & Zhou, 2021; Zhang, 2017a, 2017b).

Regarding study quality indexed by task reliability, the mean task reliabilities of the selected studies fell between the 25th and 50th percentiles when compared to second language acquisition research in general.

Before we conducted the meta-analytic analysis reported in the next section, we reassessed whether there was sufficient evidence for the various relationship outcomes (as shown in Table 2). Although Valentine and colleagues (2010) suggested that a minimum of two studies is needed for any meta-analysis, this suggestion should be evaluated with consideration of the number of independent study samples for subsequent subgroup and meta-regression analyses, which we also did for the present meta-analysis. According to Cuijpers and colleagues (2021), a subgroup analysis requires three to four times the number of studies needed for the main analysis to have sufficient power. For instance, for a two-level categorical moderator analysis, Melby-Lervåg and Lervåg (2011) included a minimum of seven independent study samples. Regarding meta-regression analysis, a minimum of ten primary studies is expected based on the rule of thumb proposed by Borenstein and colleagues (2009). In this regard, our meta-analysis only focused on the relationships between the various facets of metalinguistic awareness and word decoding in child L2 readers.

4 A Meta-Analysis of the Transfer Facilitation Effects of L1 Phonological, Orthographic, and Morphological Awareness in L2 Word Decoding

4.1 Guided Questions

The following meta-analysis focuses on the cross-language transfer of metalinguistic awareness between two languages, the intralingual contributions of metalinguistic awareness in L1 and L2 word decoding respectively, and the interlingual contributions of L1 metalinguistic awareness to L2 word decoding. Four questions were posed:

1. To what extent do L1 phonological, orthographic, and morphological awareness correlate with L2 phonological, orthographic, and morphological awareness in L2 readers?
2. To what extent do phonological, orthographic, and morphological awareness correlate with word decoding intralingually in L2 readers?
   a) To what extent do L1 phonological, orthographic, and morphological awareness correlate with L1 word decoding in L2 readers?

b) To what extent do L2 phonological, orthographic, and morphological awareness correlate with L2 word decoding in L2 readers?

3. To what extent do L1 phonological, orthographic, and morphological awareness correlate with L2 word decoding in L2 readers?

4. To what extent do the relations in Questions 1–3 vary as a function of linguistic-, learner-, measurement-, and instruction-related factors (i.e., L1–L2 writing system type, L2 proficiency, grade level/age, language majority/minority group, the measurement of phonological awareness, orthographic awareness, morphological awareness or word decoding, and medium of instruction)[9]?

4.2 Coding of Effect Sizes and Moderator Variables

Effect size coding was based on the zero-order correlation matrix (i.e., Pearson's *r* in selected studies). For the primary study of a longitudinal design, only time-one correlations were recorded to avoid interdependence. Because it is common to find multiple measures of the same construct, we used the arithmetic mean of effect sizes (after recent meta-analyses such as Branum-Martin et al., 2012; Peng et al., 2021; Ruan et al., 2018). For moderator coding, details are as follows:

L1–L2 Writing System Type. Whether both L1 and L2 writing systems were alphabet or at least one language was non-alphabet was coded (after Melby-Lervåg & Lervåg, 2011).

L2 Proficiency. Participants who were identified as beginning-level students or in the first two years of L2 learning were coded as Basic and the rest as Beyond Basic (after Jeon & Yamashita, 2014).

Grade Level/Age. The exact grade levels and age in months were coded.

Language Group Membership. There were two groups: language minority group whose L1 was not the societal language versus language majority group.

Phonological Awareness, Orthographic Awareness and Morphological Awareness Measurement. For the respective three facets of metalinguistic awareness, we coded whether previous studies used multiple measures or a single measure only.

Word Decoding Measurement. Two moderators were coded: 1) standardized design versus researcher designed; 2) word status (i.e., real words or both real

---

[9] Given the modest primary study pool of this meta-analysis, we did not conduct moderator analysis of construct-related factors. Pertinent discussion can be found in Sections 2.3 and 3.4 instead.

and pseudowords). Since all of the selected studies measured word decoding accuracy only without including word decoding fluency or efficiency, no relevant moderator analysis was conducted for this measurement factor.

Medium of Instruction. Two categories were coded: using L1 as the medium of instruction or using L2 as the medium of instruction.

4.3 Meta-Analytic Procedures

All data analyses were conducted with Comprehensive Meta-Analysis (CMA) software Version 3.0 (www.metaanalysis.com/) and Microsoft Excel. The meta-analysis included seven major steps:

First, to examine the overall correlations, an average of the correlations of all primary studies weighted for the sample sizes was calculated using an estimation of the inverse variance of each effect size (see Borenstein et al., 2009).

Second, data analysis was based on random-effects models, which according to Borenstein and colleagues (2007) are a more plausible match than fixed-effect models.

Third, to investigate variability among the correlations across primary studies, heterogeneity tests (Q test; Hedges & Olkin, 1985) were conducted. A significant value in the heterogeneity test would provide evidence for variability among the correlations (i.e., I^2 indicates the proportion of the heterogeneity that is real rather than due to chance and the parameter τ^2 indicates the variance in true effect sizes).

Fourth, given that most of the moderator variables in this study are categorical, a heterogeneity test (Q test) was performed based on mixed-effects modeling, both within and across the subgroups created by the moderator analyses. A statistically significant difference between subgroups would suggest the moderator influences the mean correlation. The analysis of potential moderators indicates whether subgroup membership affects the correlational outcomes. Notably, in addition to the moderator analyses with grade level as a categorical variable via subgroup analyses, we also examined age (in months) as a continuous variable via meta-regression analyses and compared the results. The rationale for comparing grade level and age is that the age range might vary for the same grade among different bilingual and bicultural educational settings.

Fifth, for cases where there was only one sample for a specific subgroup, we conducted a sensitivity analysis and removed one sample at a time from each moderator analysis to determine if the results would be altered. All sensitivity analyses results can be found in Appendix S4 available online at: osf.io/4z6mw.

Sixth, after significant moderator effects were identified, meta-regression analyses were conducted for any relationships with at least ten primary studies (based on the rule of thumb proposed by Borenstein et al., 2009) to identify the proportion of variance explained by the moderator(s).

Last, we examined possible effects of publication bias. Among the nineteen independent samples, sixteen were selected from published journal articles, two were based on book chapters, and one was based on an unpublished doctoral dissertation. Funnel plots for random-effects models were used to determine the presence of retrieval bias, for which the funnel would be asymmetric (see Appendix S5 online: osf.io/4z6mw). The results of Duval and Tweedie's trim and fill are reported in Tables 4 to 7 when asymmetries were found in the funnel plots.

4.4 Cross-Language Transfer between L1 and L2 Phonological, Orthographic, and Morphological Awareness

As mentioned earlier, the interpretation of effect sizes (*r*s) is based on Plonsky and Oswald's (2014) estimates for small, medium, and large correlations ($r = .25, .40, .60$, respectively). Regarding the observed variance in primary studies indexed by I^2, 25 percent, 50 percent, and 75 percent might be considered as low, moderate, and high (Borenstein et al., 2009).

For guided Question 1, Table 4 and Figures 2a to 2c illustrate that the overall mean correlation between L1 and L2 phonological awareness ($k = 7$, $N = 782$) was medium and significant, $r = .44$, 95% CI [.28, .57], $z(6) = 5.14$, $p < .001$; whereas the respective mean correlations between L1 and L2 orthographic awareness ($k = 8$, $N = 858$) and between L1 and L2 morphological awareness ($k = 8$, $N = 811$) were both small yet significant ($r = .30$, 95% CI [.08, .49], $z(7) = 2.65$, $p = .008$; $r = .28$, 95% CI [.22, .35], $z(7) = 8.15$, $p < .001$). The adjusted effect estimate results did not change our conclusions of the correlation strengths (see Table 4).

Heterogeneity test results indicated that there was significant and large variability in the correlations between L1 and L2 phonological awareness ($Q(5) = 33.54$, $p < .001$, $I^2 = 82.11\%$, $\tau^2 = .05$) as well as between L1 and L2 orthographic awareness ($Q(6) = 76.44$, $p < .001$, $I^2 = 90.84\%$, $\tau^2 = .10$). However, no significant variation was observed in the correlations between L1 and L2 morphological awareness ($Q(6) = 5.68$, $p = .578$, $I^2 < .001$, $\tau^2 < .001$).

Thus, the answer to Question 1 is that there was a significant and moderate correlation between L1 and L2 phonological awareness, whereas there were significant and small correlations between L1 and L2 orthographic awareness as well as between L1 and L2 morphological awareness.

Table 4 Mean correlations for L1 and L2 metalinguistic awareness.

Outcome	k	r[95% CI]	z(p)	Qtest[a] (p)	I^2 (%)	τ^2	Adjusted effect estimate[b]	No. of trimmed studies
L1 PA–L2 PA	7	.44 [.28, .57]	5.14 (<.001)	33.54 (<.001)	82.11	.05	N.A.	0
L1 OA–L2 OA	8	.30 [.08, .49]	2.65 (=.008)	76.44 (<.001)	90.84	.10	.28 [.23, .35]	To right of mean (k = 1)
L1 MA–L2 MA	8	.28 [.22, .35]	8.15 (<.001)	5.68 (.578)	<.001	<.001	.30 [.24, .36]	To left of mean (k = 1)

Notes. L1 = first language; L2 = second language; PA = phonological awareness; OA = orthographic awareness; MA = morphological awareness; N.A. = not applicable; [a]Heterogeneity test. [b]After trim and fill (random-effects model).

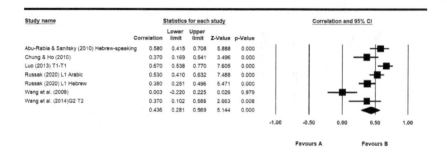

Figures 2a Forest plot of the relationship between first-language (L1) and second-language (L2) phonological awareness (PA). The results for the overall mean correlation are given in the last line.

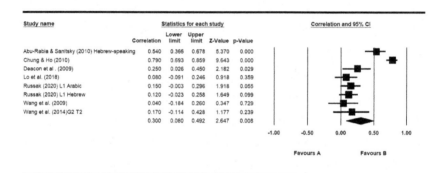

Figure 2b Forest plot of the relationship between first-language (L1) and second-language (L2) orthographic awareness (OA). The results for the overall mean correlation are given in the last line.

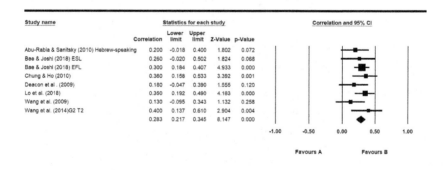

Figure 2c Forest plot of the relationship between first language (L1) and second language (L2) morphological awareness (MA). The results for the overall mean correlation are given in the last line.

4.5 Intralingual Relationships between Metalinguistic (Phonological, Orthographic, Morphological) Awareness and Word Decoding in L1

In this section, we focus on the intralingual correlations between metalinguistic (phonological, orthographic, and morphological) awareness and word decoding in bilingual readers' L1. This answers guided Question 2a. The results in Table 5 and Figures 3a to 3c indicate that, for all three relationships, the correlations were significant and small. The mean correlation between L1 phonological awareness and L1 word decoding was .27 ($k = 11$, $N = 1,239$, 95% CI [.22, .32], $z(10) = 9.43$, $p < .001$); the overall mean correlation between L1 orthographic awareness and L1 word decoding was .34 ($k = 11$, $N = 1,239$, 95% CI [.15, .50], $z(10) = 3.50$, $p < .001$); and the mean correlation between L1 morphological awareness and L1 word decoding was .38 ($k = 11$, $N = 1,239$, 95% CI [.30, .45], $z(10) = 8.78$, $p < .001$). The adjusted effect estimate results did not change our conclusions of the correlation strengths (as illustrated in Table 5).

In addition, no significant variation among primary studies was identified for the relationship between L1 phonological awareness and L1 word decoding ($Q(9) = 10.31$, $p = .414$, $I^2 = 2.97$, $\tau^2 < .001$), whereas significant large and moderate variation was found respectively for the relationship between L1 orthographic awareness and L1 word decoding ($Q(9) = 78,30$, $p < .001$, $I^2 = 89.78$, $\tau^2 = .08$), as well as the relationship between L1 morphological awareness and L1 word decoding ($Q(9) = 23.16$, $p = .010$, $I^2 = 56.81$, $\tau^2 = .01$).

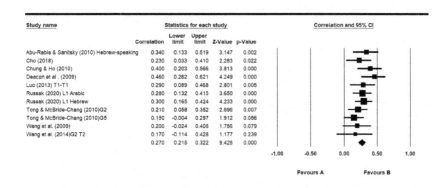

Figure 3a Forest plot of the relationship between first-language (L1) phonological awareness (PA) and word decoding (WD). The results for the overall mean correlation are given in the last line.

Table 5 Mean correlations for L1 outcomes.

Outcome	k	r [95% CI]	z (p)	Q test[a] (p)	I² (%)	τ²	Adjusted effect estimate[b]	No. of trimmed studies
L1 PA–L1 WD	11	.27 [.22, .32]	9.43 (< .001)	10.31 (=.414)	2.97	<.001	N.A.	0
L1 OA–L1 WD	11	.34 [.15, .50]	3.50 (< .001)	78.30 (<.001)	89.78	.08	.30 [.25, .35]	To right of mean (k=2)
L1 MA–L1 WD	11	.38 [.30, .45]	8.78 (< .001)	23.16 (=.010)	56.81	0.01	.39 [.35, .44]	To right of mean (k=2)

Notes. L1 = first language; PA = phonological awareness; OA = orthographic awareness; MA = morphological awareness; WD = word decoding; N.A. = not applicable. [a]Heterogeneity test. [b]After trim and fill (random-effects model).

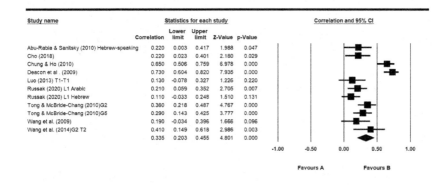

Figure 3b Forest plot of the relationship between first-language (L1) orthographic awareness (OA) and word decoding (WD). The results for the overall mean correlation are given in the last line.

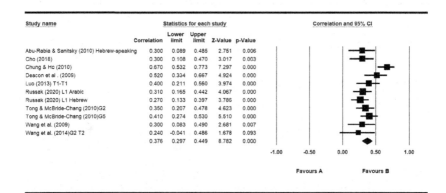

Figure 3c Forest plot of the relationship between first-language (L1) morphological awareness (MA) and word decoding (WD). The results for the overall mean correlation are given in the last line.

In response to Question 2a, we found that L1 phonological, orthographic, and morphological awareness all correlated significantly with L1 word decoding in bilingual child readers and the mean correlation magnitudes were all small.

4.6 Intralingual Relationships between Metalinguistic (Phonological, Orthographic, and Morphological) Awareness and Word Decoding in L2

This section is guided by Question 2b, that is, "To what extent do L2 phonological, orthographic, and morphological awareness correlate with L2 word decoding in L2 readers?" All three facets of metalinguistic

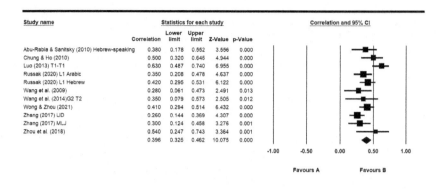

Figure 4a Forest plot of the relationship between second-language (L2) phonological awareness (PA) and word decoding (WD). The results for the .overall mean correlation are given in the last line.

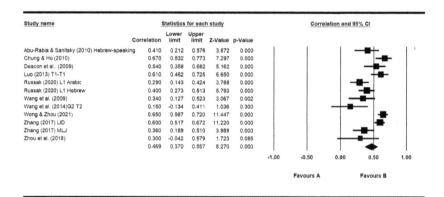

Figure 4b Forest plot of the relationship between second-language (L2) orthographic awareness (OA) and word decoding (WD). The results for the overall mean correlation are given in the last line.

awareness correlated significantly and moderately with word decoding in bilingual readers' L2: 1) The overall mean correlation between L2 phonological awareness and L2 word decoding was .40 ($k = 11, N = 1,153$, 95% CI [.33, .46], $z(10) = 10.08, p < .001$). 2) The mean correlation between L2 orthographic awareness and L2 word decoding was .47 ($k = 12, N = 1,374$, 95% CI [.37, .56], $z(11) = 8.27, p < .001$). 3) The mean correlation between L2 morphological awareness and L2 word decoding was .46 ($k = 10, N = 1,096$, 95% CI [36, .54], $z(9) = 8.35, p < .001$) (see Table 6 and Figures 4a to 4c).

Notably, heterogeneity tests were all significant for the three L2 intralingual relationships. Specifically, the variations were both moderate for the relationship

Table 6 Mean correlations for L2 outcomes.

Outcome	k	r [95% CI]	z (p)	Q test[a] (p)	I² (%)	τ²	Adjusted effect estimate[b]	No. of trimmed studies
L2 PA–L2 WD	11	.40 [.33, .46]	10.08 (<.001)	20.85 (=.022)	52.04	.01	N.A.	0
L2 OA–L2 WD	12	.47 [.37, .56]	8.27 (<.001)	54.04 (<.001)	79.64	.03	N.A.	0
L2 MA–L2 WD	10	.46 [.36, .54]	8.35 (<.001)	29.80 (<.001)	69.80	.02	N.A.	0

Notes. L2 = second language; PA = phonological awareness; OA = orthographic awareness; MA = morphological awareness; WD = word decoding; N.A. = not applicable. [a]Heterogeneity test. [b]After trim and fill (random-effects model).

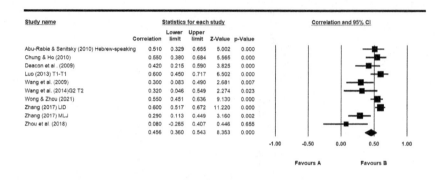

Figure 4c Forest plot of the relationship between second-language (L2) morphological awareness (MA) and word decoding (WD). The results for the overall mean correlation are given in the last line.

between L2 phonological awareness and L2 word decoding ($Q(9) = 20.85$, $p = .022$, $I^2 = 52.04$, $\tau^2 = .01$), as well as between L2 morphological awareness and L2 word decoding ($Q(8) = 29.80$, $p < .001$, $I^2 = 69.80$, $\tau^2 = .02$). There was large variation for the relationship between L2 orthographic awareness and L2 word decoding ($Q(10) = 54.04$, $p < .001$, $I^2 = 79.64$, $\tau^2 = .03$).

In response to Question 2b, there were significant and moderate correlations between L2 metalinguistic (phonological, morphological, and orthographic) awareness and L2 word decoding.

4.7 Interlingual Relationships between L1 Metalinguistic (Phonological, Orthographic, and Morphological) Awareness and L2 Word Decoding

For guided Question 3, Table 7 and Figures 5a to 5c illustrate the results of the overall mean correlations between L1 metalinguistic (phonological, orthographic, and morphological) awareness and L2 word decoding. All relationships were significant ($ps < .05$). For the relationship between L1 phonological awareness and L2 word decoding, the mean correlation (r) was .39 ($k = 10$, $N = 1,239$, 95% CI [.31, .47], $z(9) = 8.54$, $p < .001$). Notably, the adjusted effect estimate was .44 (95% CI [.39, .48]) after trim and fill, which indicated a moderate effect size. The mean correlations between L1 orthographic awareness and L2 word decoding as well as between L1 morphological awareness and L2 word decoding were both small: The respective rs were .34 ($k = 9$, $N = 1,050$, 95% CI [.15, .50], $z(8) = 3.50$, $p < .001$) and .33 ($k = 11$, $N = 1,141$, 95% CI [.33, .42], $z(10) = 6.20$, $p < .001$). The adjusted effect estimate for L1 orthographic awareness and L2 word decoding was .40 (95% CI [.35, .45]) after trim and fill, which indicated a moderate correlation.

Table 7 Mean correlations for L1 metalinguistic awareness and L2 word decoding.

Outcome	k	r [95% CI]	z (p)	Q test[a] (p)	I² (%)	τ²	Adjusted effect estimate[b]	No. of trimmed studies
L1 PA–L2 WD	10	.39 [.31, .47]	8.54 (<.001)	22.18 (=.008)	59.43	.01	.44 [.39, .48]	To right of mean (k = 2)
L1 OA–L2 WD	9	.34 [.15, .50]	3.50 (<.001)	78.30 (<.001)	89.78	.08	.40 [.35, .45]	To right of mean (k = 2)
L1 MA–L2 WD	11	.33 [.33, .42]	6.20 (<.001)	34.32 (<.001)	70.87	.02	N.A.	0

Notes. L1 = first language; L2 = second language; PA = phonological awareness; OA = orthographic awareness; MA = morphological awareness; WD = word decoding; N.A. = not applicable. [a]Heterogeneity test. [b]After trim and fill (random-effects model).

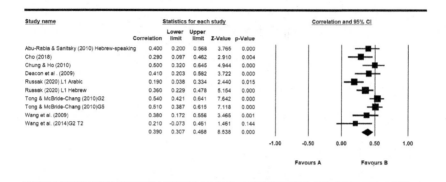

Figure 5a Forest plot of the relationship between first-language (L1) phonological awareness (PA) and second-language (L2) word decoding (WD). The results for the overall mean correlation are given in the last line.

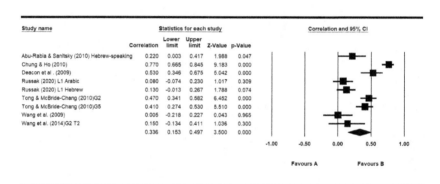

Figure 5b Forest plot of the relationship between first-language (L1) orthographic awareness (OA) and second language (L2) word decoding (WD). The results for the overall mean correlation are given in the last line.

Heterogeneity tests were significant and small for the relationship between L1 phonological awareness and L2 word decoding ($Q(8) = 22.18$, $p < .001$, $I^2 = 59.43$, $\tau^2 = .01$); significant and small for the relationship between L1 morphological awareness and L2 word decoding ($Q(7) = 34.32$, $p < .001$, $I^2 = 70.87$, $\tau^2 = .08$); and significant and large for the relationship between L1 orthographic awareness and L2 word decoding ($Q(9) = 78.30$, $p < .001$, $I^2 = 89.78$, $\tau^2 = .02$).

In response to Question 3, there were significant and moderate correlations (after adjusted estimation) between L1 phonological awareness and L2 word decoding, and between L1 orthographic awareness and L2 word decoding, as well as a significant and small correlation between L1 morphological awareness and L2 word decoding.

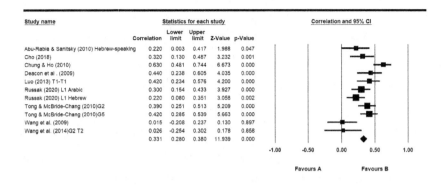

Figure 5c Forest plot of the relationship between first-language (L1) morphological awareness and second-language (L2) word decoding. The results for the overall mean correlation are given in the last line.

4.8 Moderator Analyses: Linguistic-, Learner-, Measurement-, and Instruction-Related Effects

4.8.1 Subgroup Analyses

No moderator analyses were conducted for the relationship between L1 and L2 morphological awareness or the relationship between L1 phonological awareness and L1 word decoding because no significant heterogeneity was detected (see Table 4 and Table 5). For relationships that included three subgroups (usually with one subgroup of mixed features), we conducted sensitivity analyses. For example, a sensitivity analysis was carried out for the relationship between L2 phonological awareness and L2 word decoding because one study with mixed L2 proficiency groups was removed, but the removal did not change the results. We only report significant moderating effects below (and we did not identify any significant moderating effects for the relationship between L1 and L2 phonological awareness, the relationship between L1 morphological awareness and L1 word decoding, the relationship between L2 orthographic awareness and L2 word decoding, the relationship between L2 morphological awareness and L2 word decoding, or the relationship between L1 phonological awareness and L2 word decoding).

Table 8 illustrates the subgroup analysis results for the relationships between L1 and L2 metalinguistic (orthographic) awareness. The results indicated that the number of orthographic measures (i.e., single vs. multiple) was a significant moderator ($Q = 8.96$, $p = 0.003$). The mean correlation of primary studies using a single measure of orthographic awareness was small ($r = .13$, $k = 6$), yet the mean correlation was large for primary studies using multiple measures of orthographic awareness ($r = .69$, $k = 2$).

Table 8 Moderator analysis results for the relationships between L1 and L2 metalinguistic (orthographic) awareness.

Outcome	Moderator	Moderator variable	No. of correlations (k)	r	95% CI (r)	r difference	Q test[a]
L1 OA–L2 OA	OA measure	Single	6	.13	.05, .20	–.56	8.96 (p = .003)
		Multiple	2	.69	.36, .86		

Notes. L1 = first language; L2 = second language; OA = orthographic awareness. [a] Heterogeneity test.

There were two major findings regarding moderating effects on the intralingual relationships between metalinguistic (phonological and orthographic) awareness and word decoding in L1 or L2 (as shown in Table 9): 1) Word decoding task design (i.e., standardized vs. researcher-designed) had a significant moderating effect on the relationship between L1 orthographic awareness and L1 word decoding (Q = 7.21, p = 0.007) and the mean correlation was larger in primary studies using standardized word decoding measures (r difference = .27). 2) L2 proficiency was a significant moderator for the relationship between L2 phonological awareness and L2 word decoding (Q = 7.33, p = 0.007), with a larger correlation for the basic L2 proficiency group (r difference = .16).

Lastly, for the interlingual relationships between L1 metalinguistic (orthographic and morphological) awareness and L2 word decoding, two significant moderators were identified: language group membership, and word status in word decoding tasks (ps < .05, as shown in the Q test results in Table 10). For the interlingual relationship between L1 orthographic awareness and L2 word decoding, the mean correlations were smaller in the language minority group than in the language majority group. For the relationship between L1 morphological awareness and L2 word decoding, the mean correlation of primary studies using real words only in the word decoding measures was larger than that using both real and pseudowords.

4.8.2 Meta-Regression Analyses

After significant moderator effects were identified, meta-regression analyses were conducted for three relationships in a minimum of ten primary studies (based on the rule of thumb proposed by Borenstein et al., 2009): 1) L2 phonological awareness and L2 word decoding, 2) L2 orthographic awareness and L2 word decoding, and 3) L1 morphological awareness and L2 word decoding.

For all four relationships, we conducted moderator analyses with age as a continuous variable and compared the results with those with grade level as a categorical variable. Grade level was not found to be a significant moderator for any of the relationships examined in Section 4.7; however, as a continuous variable, age in months was a significant moderator for the relationship between L2 phonological awareness and L2 word decoding (β = −0.004, p = .035, R^2 = 0.37; see Model 1 in Table 11). As Figure 6 illustrates, as age increased, the strength of the relationship between L2 phonological awareness and L2 word decoding decreased. No moderating effect of age on other relationships was found.

For the relationship between L2 phonological awareness and L2 word decoding, we also identified L2 proficiency (basic vs. beyond basic) as

Table 9 Moderator analysis results for the intralingual relationships between metalinguistic (phonological and orthographic) awareness and word decoding in L1 and L2.

Outcome	Moderator	Moderator variable	No. of correlations (*k*)	*r*	95% CI (*r*)	*r* difference	*Q* test[a]
L1 OA–L1 WD	WD design	Standardized	7	.43	.26, .58	.27	7.21 (*p* = .007)
		Researcher-designed	4	.16	.08, .25		
L2 PA–L2 WD	L2 proficiency	Basic	6	.44	.36, .52	.16	7.33 (*p* = .007)
		Beyond basic	4	.28	.20, .36		

Notes. L1 = first language; L2 = second language; PA = phonological awareness; OA = orthographic awareness. [a] Heterogeneity test.

Table 10 Moderator analysis results for the interlingual relationships between L1 metalinguistic (orthographic and morphological) awareness and L2 word decoding.

Outcome	Moderator	Moderator variable	No. of correlations (k)	r	95% CI (r)	r difference	Q test[a]
L1 OA–L2 WD	Language group membership	Minority	3	.07	−.04, .19	−.42	9.42 ($p = .002$)
		Majority	5	.49	.26, .66		
L1 MA–L2 WD	WD word status	Real words	9	.37	.29, .45	.35	13.17 ($p < .001$)
		Real and pseudo words	2	.02	−.16, .19		

Notes. L1 = first language; L2 = second language; OA = orthographic awareness; MA = morphological awareness. [a] Heterogeneity test.

Table 11 Meta-regression analysis results with age and L2 proficiency as covariates for the relationship between L2 phonological awareness and L2 word decoding ($k = 10$).

Covariate	Coefficient	Standard error	95% lower	95% upper	Z-value	p	R^2
Model 1							
Intercept	0.804	0.223	0.367	1.242	3.60	<.001	
Age	−0.004	0.002	−0.007	0.0003	−1.82	.035	0.37
Model 2							
Intercept	0.480	0.047	0.387	0.572	10.18	<.001	
L2 proficiency (beyond basic)	−0.186	0.073	−0.328	−0.044	−2.56	.005	.71
Model 3							
Intercept	0.888	0.176	0.543	1.233	5.04	<.001	
Age	−0.004	0.002	−0.007	−0.001	−2.44	.007	
L2 proficiency (beyond basic)	−0.181	0.059	−0.297	−3.080	−3.08	.001	1.00
Model 4							
Intercept	0.888	0.176	0.543	1.233	5.04	<.001	
L2 proficiency (beyond basic)	−0.181	0.059	−0.297	−0.066	−3.08	.001	
Age	−0.004	0.002	−0.007	−0.001	−2.44	.007	1.00

Notes. L2 = second language. For the "L2 proficiency" moderator, there are two categories (basic vs. beyond basic); the basic L2 proficiency group was treated as the reference group. CMA V3 software automatically generated dummy coding for the categorical moderator.

Figure 6 Scatter plot of the moderating effect of age on the relationship between second-language (L2) phonological awareness and second-language (L2) word decoding.

a significant moderator ($\beta = -0.186$, $p = .005$, $R^2 = 0.71$, as shown in Model 2 in Table 11). As L2 proficiency increased, the magnitude of the relationship between L2 phonological awareness and L2 word decoding decreased. When both age and L2 proficiency were entered for meta-regression in reverse order, each had an additional effect over the other (as shown in Model 3 and Model 4 in Table 11). The variance was completely explained by the two moderators ($R^2 = 1.00$).

Table 12 illustrates the meta-regression analysis results for the relationship between L2 orthographic awareness and L2 word decoding. When language group membership was entered into the meta-regression model, it had a significant effect, thereby explaining the variance of the correlation between L2 orthographic awareness and L2 word decoding ($R^2 = .28$). According to Plonsky and Ghanbar (2018), an R^2 less than .10 or .18 is considered as small or moderate, and regression models explaining more than 50 percent of the variance are considered fairly robust. In the case of this study, the moderating effect of language group membership on the relationship between L2 orthographic awareness and L2 word decoding was moderate.

Finally, we also examined the moderating effect of word status in word-decoding measures on the relationship between L1 morphological awareness and L2 word decoding. As Table 13 indicates, when it was entered into the meta-regression model, "word-decoding word status" had a significant effect explaining the variance of the correlation between L1 morphological awareness and L2 word decoding (respective $R^2 = 0.56$), thereby making it a robust finding.

Table 12 Meta-regression analysis results for the relationship between L2 orthographic awareness and L2 word decoding ($k = 12$).

Model Covariate	Coefficient	Standard error	95% lower	95% upper	Z-value	p	R^2
Intercept	0.376	0.091	0.197	0.555	4.12	< .001	0.28
Language group membership (majority)	0.237	0.119	0.005	0.470	2.00	.023	

Note. For the moderator "language group membership," there are two categories (minority vs. majority); the language minority group was treated as the reference group.

Table 13 Meta-regression analysis results for the relationship between L1 morphological awareness and L2 word decoding ($k = 10$).

Model Covariate	Coefficient	Standard error	95% lower	95% upper	Z-value	p	R^2
Intercept	0.409	0.049	0.313	0.506	8.34	< .001	
word-decoding word status	−0.390	0.127	−0.639	−0.141	−3.06	= .001	0.56

Note. For the moderator "word-decoding word status," there are two categories (real words vs. real and pseudowords); the real word group was treated as the reference group.

In response to Question 4, "to what extent do the relations above (in Questions 1–3) vary as a function of linguistic-, learner-, measurement- and instruction-related factors (i.e., L1–L2 writing system type, language majority/ minority group, L2 proficiency, grade level/age, the measurement of phono- logical awareness, orthographic awareness, morphological awareness, or word decoding, and medium of instruction)," there were five major findings:

1. The L1–L2 writing system type did not have any significant moderating effects.
2. We also found that the variance in the correlation between L2 orthographic awareness and L2 word decoding was significantly moderated by language group membership. The relationship was stronger for the language major- ity group.
3. The variance in the correlation between L2 phonological awareness and L2 word decoding can be explained by age and L2 proficiency ($R^2 = 1.00$). As age and L2 proficiency increased, the strength of the relationship decreased. However, due to the small independent sample size, we could not analyze any interactional effects between age and L2 proficiency. Notably, we examined potential moderating effects of grade level as a categorical vari- able (kindergarten to grade two vs. grade three and above) versus age as a continuous variable, and found no significant moderating effect of grade level. In contrast, a significant moderating effect of age on the relationship between L2 phonological awareness and L2 word decoding was observed.
4. We observed a significant moderating effect of orthographic awareness measurement on the relationship between L1 and L2 orthographic aware- ness based on subgroup analysis, with a larger mean correlation in primary studies using multiple measures. We also found that "word-decoding word status" had a robust effect explaining the variance of the correlation between L1 morphological awareness and L2 word decoding, and the correlation was higher for *real* word decoding.
5. No significant moderating effects of medium of instruction were detected.

4.9 General Discussion: A Comparison of Results between This Meta-Analysis and Prior Meta-Analytic Reviews

Transfer of Metalinguistic Awareness. The findings of different magnitudes of mean correlations among the three facets of metalinguistic awareness (i.e., a moderate effect size for phonological awareness as well as small effect sizes for orthographic and morphological awareness) seem to be consistent with Koda's (2005, 2008) conceptualizations of phonological awareness as a language-general facet of metalinguistic awareness versus orthographic and morphological awareness as language-specific facets of metalinguistic awareness (see also Chung et al., 2019; Koda et al., 2014; Perfetti, 2003). In previous meta-analyses with larger independent sample pools, Melby-Lervåg and Lervåg (2011), for example, observed a large and significant mean correlation between L1 and L2 phonological awareness ($r = .60$, 95% CI [.49, .69], $k = 16$, $N = 1,340$, z (15) = 58.50, $p = 0.01$). In addition, Ke and colleagues' (2021) meta-analysis of morphological awareness in child biliteracy development found a small correlation between L1 and L2 morphological awareness ($r = .30$, 95% CI [.22, .38], $k = 20$, $N = 1,657$, $z(19) = 7.14$, $p < .001$). To our knowledge, our meta-analysis is among the first to provide aggregative evidence of the significant and small correlation between L1 and L2 orthographic awareness ($r = .30$). This has filled a notable gap in previous meta-analyses of metalinguistic awareness and reading.

Intralingual Relationship between Metalinguistic Awareness and Word Decoding in L1. The comparison results are summarized in Table 14, which indicates significant variation in the meta-analytic results for the relationship between L1 phonological awareness and L1 word decoding, ranging from small to moderate for bilingual readers of mixed L1s (as shown by the results of this meta-analysis), L1 Chinese readers (see Ruan et al., 2018), or Spanish readers with monolingual and bilingual backgrounds (see Míguez-Álvarez et al., 2021). Specifically, for L1 English monolingual readers, the correlation between L1 phonological awareness and word decoding appeared to be higher (above the moderate level or .40) according to Ruan and colleagues (2018). With respect to the relationship between L1 morphological awareness and L1 word decoding, both this meta-analysis and that of Ruan and colleagues suggested that the magnitude was close to the moderate range (i.e., .40).

Regarding the relationship between L1 orthographic awareness and L1 word decoding, to the best of our knowledge there is only one meta-analytic review in the existing literature (Georgiou et al., 2021). In their research, Georgiou et al. analyzed sixty-eight studies, the majority of which were about reading English as the target language. They found that there were significant differences between dyslexic readers against a chronological age control group and a reading level control group, and that the significant heterogeneity in the effect sizes was partly explained by the level of orthographic knowledge (larger effect sizes were observed at the lexical level than at the sublexical level). Based on a relatively small sample size ($k = 9$), our meta-analytic results suggested that orthographic awareness, like phonological and morphological awareness, correlated significantly with word decoding in bilingual children's L1 reading and that the effect size was small ($r = .34$).

Table 14 Comparisons of L1-related effect sizes between this meta-analysis and previous meta-analyses.

Study	Outcome	Population and language	k	r estimate
This meta-analysis	L1 PA–L1 WD	Bilingual children; mixed L1s	11	.27
Míguez-Álvarez et al. (2021)[a]	L1 PA–L1 WD	The majority were monolingual Spanish speakers; L1 Spanish	Range: 9 to 39	Range: .29 to .42
Ruan et al. (2018)[b]	L1 PA–L1 WD	Monolinguals; L1 English	Range: 11 to 41	Range: .51 to .55
Ruan et al. (2018)	L1 PA–L1 WD	Monolinguals; L1 Chinese	Range: 6 to 41	Range: .26 to .30
This meta-analysis	L1 MA–L1 WD	Bilingual children; mixed L1s	11	.38
Ruan et al. (2018)	L1 MA–L1 WD	Monolinguals; L1 English	Range: 11 to 41	Range: .37 to .46
Ruan et al. (2018)	L1 MA–L1 WD	Monolinguals; L1 Chinese	Range: 6 to 41	.39

Notes. L1 = first language; PA = phonological awareness; MA = morphological awareness; WD = word decoding. [a]Míguez-Álvarez and colleagues (2021) examined three facets of phonological awareness (i.e., phonemic, intrasyllabic, and syllabic awareness) and two measures of word decoding (i.e., real and nonword decoding). [b]Ruan and colleagues (2018) included two measures of word decoding (i.e., accuracy and fluency).

Intralingual Relationship between Metalinguistic Awareness and Word Decoding in L2. For comparison purposes, we tried to identify related effect sizes from previous meta-analyses of phonological awareness and word decoding in bilingual/L2 readers (e.g., Branum-Martin et al., 2012; Jeon & Yamashita, 2014; Melby-Lervåg & Lervåg, 2011). However, the relationship between L2 phonological awareness and L2 word reading was not examined in those meta-analyses. One exception is Míguez-Álvarez and colleagues' (2021) meta-analysis of Spanish phonological awareness in a sample comprised mainly of monolingual Spanish-speaking children and mixed with L2 Spanish-speaking children whose L1s were Aymara, Basque, or English. Míguez-Álvarez and colleagues found a stronger correlation between phonological awareness and word decoding in bilingual children than in monolingual children. Similarly, in the present meta-analysis, we found a larger correlation between phonological awareness and word decoding in bilingual readers' L2 ($r = .46$ within the moderate effect size range) than in their L1 ($r = .27$ within the small effect size range).

Regarding the strength of the relationship between L2 morphological awareness and L2 word decoding, both this meta-analysis (albeit it having a small sample size, $k = 10$) and Ke and colleagues (2021) ($k = 34$) identified an overall mean (r) of .46. Lastly, we could not identify any meta-analysis of orthographic awareness and word decoding in L2 reading in the existing literature. Our results suggested a moderate correlation between L2 orthographic awareness and L2 word decoding ($r = .47$, $k = 12$).

Cross-Language Transfer Facilitation Relationships between L1 Metalinguistic Awareness and L2 Word Decoding. When comparing our effect sizes with those in previous metanalyses (see Table 15), we found that both this meta-analysis and previous ones suggested a moderate range of correlation between L1 phonological awareness and L2 word decoding as well as a small correlation between L1 morphological awareness and L2 word decoding. No comparison could be drawn in previous meta-analyses regarding the correlations between L1 orthographic awareness and L2 word decoding, but this meta-analysis found a medium correlation based on adjusted estimation ($r = .40$, $k = 11$).

Linguistic-, Learner-, Measurement-, and Instruction-Related Moderating Effects. To recapitulate, a range of moderator factors was examined in this meta-analysis, including L1–L2 writing system type; L2 proficiency; grade level/age; language majority/minority group; measurements of phonological, orthographic, and morphological awareness or word decoding; and medium of instruction.

Table 15 Comparisons of L1-related effect sizes between this meta-analyses and previous meta-analyses.

Study	Outcome	Population and language	k	r estimate
This meta-analysis	L1 PA– L2 WD	Bilingual children; mixed L1s	10	.44[a]
Melby-Lervåg & Lervåg (2011)	L1 PA– L2 WD	Bilingual children; mixed L1s	14	.44
This meta-analysis	L1 MA– L2 WD	Bilingual children; mixed L1s	11	.33
Ke et al. (2021)	L1 MA– L2 WD	Bilingual children; mixed L1s	19	.35

Note. L1 = first language; L2 = second language; PA = phonological awareness; MA = morphological awareness; WD = word decoding. [a]This value was based on an adjusted effect estimate.

Neither this meta-analysis nor previous ones (e.g., Ke et al., 2021; Melby-Lervåg & Lervåg, 2011) identified any significant moderating effects of L1–L2 writing system type, thus indicating that the cross-language transfer of L1 metalinguistic awareness is not subject to L1–L2 distance. Once metalinguistic awareness is developed in L1, it is readily exploitable for L2 reading subskill acquisition. This finding applies to both language-general (phonological) and language-specific (orthographic and morphological) metalinguistic awareness. On the other hand, it could be influenced by our general operationalization of L1–L2 writing system type as a two-level categorical variable (i.e., a combination of two alphabetic languages vs. inclusion of at least one nonalphabetic language in L1 or L2). This was mainly because the target L2s for the three relationships (i.e., L1 and L2 phonological awareness, L1 and L2 orthographic awareness, and L1 and L2 morphological awareness) were either English or French in the selected studies. We thus urge future research to analyze the L1–L2 distance factor with more refined categorization. As one of the anonymous reviewers pointed out, the magnitudes of transfer facilitation effects might vary between alphabetic L1–morphosyllabic L2 readers and morphosyllabic L1–alphabetic L2 readers.

We observed significant moderating effects of age and L2 proficiency, specifically for the relationship between L2 phonological awareness and L2 word decoding. As age and L2 proficiency level increased, the correlation became weaker. Additionally, in this meta-analysis, no influence of age or L2 proficiency was observed for any of the relationships associated with orthographic or morphological awareness. Our findings, taken together, suggest that phonological awareness may play a less important role than orthographic and morphological awareness in L2 reading development in the long run. This also seems to corroborate Ke and colleagues' (2021) finding that there was a larger correlation for L2 morphological awareness and L2 reading at upper grade levels (i.e., grade three and above) than at lower grade levels (i.e., kindergarten to grade two), which suggests a sustainably important role of morphological awareness in L2 reading development.

We also found significant moderating effects of language group membership on the relationship between L2 metalinguistic awareness and L2 word decoding. Larger correlations were observed for the language majority group, which was consistent with the finding of Bratlie and colleagues' (2022) meta-analysis that mainly compared English morphological knowledge between language majority and language minority groups. The weaker relationship between metalinguistic awareness and word decoding in the language minority group could be jointly influenced by their relatively weaker foundation in L1 metalinguistic awareness sophistication and less exposure to L2 print input compared to the language majority group (see also Koda, 2005, 2008).

In regard to measurement-related effects, previous meta-analyses of phonological awareness or morphological awareness (e.g., Bratlie et al., 2022; Míguez-Álvarez et al., 2021; Ruan et al., 2018) identified larger correlations for studies using complex measures of phonological awareness and included nonword decoding and word decoding accuracy as reading outcomes. Larger correlations were also observed for those that measured oral and expressive/productive morphological awareness compared to those measuring written and receptive/judgmental morphological awareness. To add to the literature, this meta-analysis found a significant moderating effect of orthographic awareness measurement on the relationship between L1 and L2 orthographic awareness based on subgroup analysis, with a larger mean correlation in primary studies using multiple measures compared to studies using only a single measure.

Lastly, medium of instruction did not have any significant moderating effects on any of the focal relationships. This finding is similar to that of Melby-Lervåg and Lervåg's (2011) meta-analysis of phonological awareness only.

4.10 Summary

The meta-analytic analyses above focused on the cross-language correlations between three facets of metalinguistic awareness (i.e., phonological, orthographic, and morphological awareness), as well as the intralingual and interlingual relationships between metalinguistic awareness and word decoding in

2,654 bilingual children with nineteen independent samples from sixteen primary studies. Our guided research questions were not about *whether* there is any transfer of metalinguistic awareness or *how* transfer facilitation occurs; rather, we examined *to what extent* metalinguistic awareness developed in L1 correlates with corresponding L2 metalinguistic awareness and reading subskills. We also aimed to demonstrate more systematic analyses of linguistic-, learner-, measurement-, and instruction-related factors to identify significant moderators.

The findings included: 1) There was a significant and moderate correlation between L1 and L2 phonological awareness, a language-general facet of metalinguistic awareness; in contrast, there were significant and small correlations between L1 and L2 language-specific metalinguistic awareness (i.e., orthographic and morphological awareness), consistent with the predictions of the Transfer Facilitation Model (Koda, 2005, 2008). 2) There were significant and small correlations between L1 metalinguistic (phonological, morphological, and orthographic) awareness and L1 word decoding in child bilingual readers; in contrast, there were significant and moderate correlations between L2 metalinguistic (phonological, morphological, and orthographic) awareness and L2 word decoding. This result is also aligned with the Lexical Quality Hypothesis (Perfetti, 2007; Perfetti & Hart, 2002) and the Repertoire Theory of Literacy Development (Apel et al., 2004; Masterson & Apel, 2000), suggesting that all three major facets of metalinguistic awareness (i.e., phonological, orthographic, and morphological awareness) are important for both L1 and L2 word decoding. A unique finding of our meta-analysis was that metalinguistic awareness played a more important role in L2 word decoding than in L1 word decoding in child bilingual readers. 3) Interlingually speaking, there were significant and moderate correlations between L1 phonological awareness and L2 word decoding, and between L1 orthographic awareness and L2 word decoding, as well as a significant and small correlation between L1 morphological awareness and L2 word decoding. 4), Age, L2 proficiency, language group membership (i.e., majority vs. minority), as well as the measurement of orthographic awareness and word decoding had significant moderating effects. Specifically, as age and L2 proficiency level increased, the correlation strength between L2 phonological awareness and L2 word decoding decreased. Additionally, language group membership had a significant influence on the relationship between L2 orthographic awareness and L2 word decoding, and the relationships were weaker for the language minority group. Furthermore, larger correlations were observed for primary studies using multiple measures of orthographic awareness (as opposed to a single measure) and measuring word decoding with real words and standardized testing design. Finally, no significant moderating effects were identified for L1–L2 writing system type or medium instruction.

5 Concluding Remarks

5.1 Reflection

In this Element, our primary goal was to provide a comprehensive account of the complexity of metalinguistic awareness and its impacts on second-language reading development. To our knowledge, we are among the first to evaluate the roles of the three different facets of metalinguistic awareness (i.e., phonological, orthographic, and morphological awareness) simultaneously via a meta-analytic review of L2 reading studies. We began by providing brief explanations of the theoretical foundations by relating them to the Lexical Quality Hypothesis (Perfetti, 2007; Perfetti & Hart, 2002), the Repertoire Theory of Literacy Development (Apel et al., 2004; Masterson & Apel, 2000), and the Transfer Facilitation Model (Koda, 2005, 2008), clarifying the definition of metalinguistic awareness as a multifaceted construct in relation to reading development, that is, "the ability to reflect on and manipulate the structural features of language" (Nagy, 2007, p. 53; Nagy & Anderson, 1995, p. 2), and describing the possible mechanisms through which metalinguistic awareness develops reciprocally with reading competence and lexical knowledge and contributes to reading development. Subsequently, we reported a scoping review and meta-analysis of correlation coefficients with four guided questions: 1) To what extent do L1 phonological, orthographic, and morphological awareness correlate with L2 phonological, orthographic, and morphological awareness in L2 readers? 2) To what extent do phonological, orthographic, and morphological awareness correlate with word decoding intralingually in L2 readers? 3) To what extent do L1 phonological, orthographic, and morphological awareness correlate with L2 word decoding in L2 readers? 4) To what extent do the relations in Questions 1–3 vary as a function of linguistic-, learner-, measurement-, and instruction-related factors?

Based on the evidence of the present meta-analysis and previous ones reviewed in this Element (Section 2), we concluded, for Question 1, that, regardless of the distance between a learner's first and second languages, there were significant small to moderate correlations between the various facets of metalinguistic awareness in the two languages. In response to Questions 2 to 3, our meta-analysis focused on word decoding only because primary studies yielded insufficient evidence for other reading-related outcomes (e.g., lexical inferencing, vocabulary knowledge, and reading comprehension). Results indicated that there were significant correlations between the three facets of metalinguistic awareness and word decoding in both first and second languages, and metalinguistic awareness played a more important role in L2 reading than in L1 reading (see also Bialystok, 2001; Goodwin & Ahn, 2013). In addition, the meta-analytic evidence seemed to confirm the theorization that phonological awareness is a language-general facet of metalinguistic awareness, whereas orthographic and morphological awareness are language specific (Koda, 2005, 2008; Perfetti, 2003). Specifically, these conclusions were supported by the evidence that there were moderate correlations between L1 phonological awareness and L2 phonological awareness or word decoding, small correlations between L1 orthographic awareness and L2 orthographic awareness or word decoding, and small correlations between L1 morphological awareness and L2 morphological awareness or word decoding.

Finally, there was significant variation in the selected studies (i.e., sixteen primary studies that measured the three facets of metalinguistic awareness simultaneously in K–8 child bilingual learners representing twelve languages and four writing systems, mostly reading English as the target L2). Among a range of linguistic-, learner-, measurement-, and instruction-related factors tested under Question 4, we have identified five significant moderators: age, L2 proficiency, language group membership (i.e., majority vs. minority), as well as the measurement of orthographic awareness and word decoding. Another notable construct-related factor was how the selected studies defined and operationalized the three facets of metalinguistic awareness, each being a complex and multidimensional construct. Our scoping review has found that only about half the primary studies provided clear definitions of metalinguistic awareness. For studies that did not include this information, the strength of test validity (the extent to which a test measures what it is intended to measure, Kerlinger, 1999; Messick,1989) may be questionable.

We acknowledge that several limitations need to be addressed in future research. First, the evidence meta-analyzed was primarily correlational, not causal (e.g., based on empirical studies of longitudinal or interventional designs, Ke & Zhang, 2021). Second, the independent study sample size was modest and the participants were mainly child learners of L2 alphabetic languages (e.g., English and French), partly because of our strict inclusion criterion that all three facets of metalinguistic awareness should be concurrently measured in a study. There is a need in the future for a (semi-) replicated meta-analysis with a larger pool of independent study samples examining at least one facet of metalinguistic awareness and including both child and adult learners of diverse L2s. Third, due to limited independent study samples, we could not carry out meta-analyses of the relationships between L1 metalinguistic awareness and L2 lexical inferencing, reading comprehension, or vocabulary knowledge. Although our meta-analytic evidence seemed to converge on the cross-language correlations between L1 metalinguistic awareness and corresponding metalinguistic awareness and word decoding in the L2, and we could therefore possibly infer that metalinguistic awareness can indirectly facilitate reading comprehension via the mediating effects of word decoding (e.g., Badian, 2001; Deacon et al., 2014; Li & Wu, 2015; Zhang et al., 2020; Zhao et al., 2019), it is important to examine the reciprocal relationships, particularly interlingually, among metalinguistic awareness, word decoding, lexical inferencing, vocabulary knowledge, and reading comprehension via primary and meta-analytic research. Finally, caution should be taken regarding the interpretation of the five significant moderators identified in the present meta-analysis because there might be confounding effects among them (Gottardo et al., 2021). To our knowledge, it is rare for existing meta-analyses of reading or applied linguistics research to examine interactional effects of more than one moderator.

5.2 Implications for Applied Linguistics Research: A Research Agenda

There are three cross-cutting themes worthy of more in-depth research in the future:

1. *A systematic account of societal/contextual factors in addition to cognitive and linguistic factors in the development of metalinguistic awareness in relation to L2 reading.* Ever since Koda (2005, 2008) proposed the Transfer Facilitation Model of L2 reading, ample evidence has been generated from studies with L2 learners who usually have established L1 skills. Existing evidence has supported the important contentions proposed in the model (e.g., metalinguistic awareness provides a window for researching transfer; L1 transfer is nonvolitional and automatic; multiple cognitive and linguistic factors modulate transfer facilitation effects such as L1–L2 distance, L1 and L2 proficiency, and language complexity [for reviews, see Koda & Ke, 2018; Koda & Reddy, 2008]). Recent reflections on the Transfer Facilitation Model (e.g., Chung et al., 2019) have called for more attention to societal/contextual factors related to L2 reading. Some examples include, yet are not limited to, program type, teaching methods, and use of L1/L2 as dominant societal and instructional languages (see a discussion in Gottardo et al., 2021). In addition, the Transfer Facilitation Model has mainly dealt with two languages; its explanatory power remains unclear for research of multilingual or multidialectal learners of more than two languages (except an ambitious forthcoming volume entitled *Handbook of Literacy in Diglossia and in Dialectal Contexts: Psycholinguistic, Neurolinguistic, and Educational Perspectives* edited by Saiegh-Haddad et al., 2022).

2. *The causal effect of metalinguistic awareness on L2 reading development.* Two potential approaches can be used to verify the causality relationship between metalinguistic awareness and L2 reading. One is to expand current lines of longitudinal and interventional research of metalinguistic awareness instruction in L2 learners, and examine whether instruction promoting L1

metalinguistic awareness will lead to changes in L2 metalinguistic awareness and reading subskills, ideally in typologically different languages and writing systems (e.g., the transfer of English morphological awareness to Malay as a result of English morphology instruction in Zhang, 2016). In a recent review of L2 English reading research, Ke and Zhang (2021) suggested that the effects of morphological instruction delivered in English are transferrable to lexical inferencing in English and to reading development in another language. The other approach is to validate the metalinguistic hypothesis (Nagy, 2007) via meta-analyses of a multivariate nature. With recent advancement in meta-analytic methods (e.g., meta-analytic structural equation modeling, Cheung, 2014; Cheung & Chan, 2005; Jak & Cheung, 2020) and aggregative evidence of L2 reading studies, it is possible to model the reciprocal relationships among metalinguistic awareness, reading competence (including word decoding, lexical inferencing, and reading comprehension), and vocabulary knowledge to test whether metalinguistic awareness mediates the relationship between reading competence and vocabulary knowledge in L2 learners. It should be noted that since prior empirical studies tended to examine word decoding rather than reading comprehension as the focal reading outcome (as shown in Table 2), it might be premature to provide meta-analytic evidence comparing the relative contributions of different metalinguistic skills to word decoding and reading comprehension, respectively. Therefore, more attention needs to be paid to examining L2 reading comprehension as one of the target L2 reading outcomes in future research of metalinguistic awareness.

3. *Assessment of metalinguistic awareness in relation to L2 reading.* Among the three facets of metalinguistic awareness, phonological and morphological awareness assessment are relatively more established, while what constitutes orthographic awareness is still debatable (Apel, 2011; Apel et al., 2019). This may not be surprising because advances in reading psychology in recent decades have led to a focus on the linguistic aspects of reading, particularly the phonological and morphological processes involved (Share, 2021), and, unfortunately, a relative neglect of the visual processes (Berninger, 1994; see a review by Li, 2021). However, recent research of self-teaching during reading in L1 and/or L2 readers, including both children and adults, has reignited interest in orthographic learning and awareness (Li et al., 2020). Another future direction is the development of timed computerized tests of metalinguistic awareness. Since our meta-analysis sample participants were child bilingual readers, the metalinguistic awareness tests were commonly paper-and-pencil based or administered orally in a face-to-face manner. These tests recorded accuracy rates only. This

operationalization that focused on untimed task performance and accuracy seems to limit the examination of metalinguistic awareness to language analysis only, and neglect the attentional control component involved in metalinguistically demanding tasks (Bialystok, 2001; Bialystok & Ryan, 1985). Recent adult L1 and L2 reading research has begun to adopt computerized and timed tasks that tap efficiency performance (i.e., both reaction times and accuracy rates; e.g., an English morpheme counting task by Bernstein et al., 2020, and English and Chinese affix shifting tasks by Ke & Koda, 2021). These tasks have the potential to be expanded for assessment and diagnostic purposes in cognitively and linguistically diverse learner populations. Finally, this Element has only focused on three major facets of metalinguistic awareness. It may be worthwhile examining other facets of metalinguistic awareness (e.g., syntactic awareness, the ability to manipulate and reflect on the grammatical structure of language, in Brimo et al., 2017; Cain, 2007; Sohail et al., 2022; and Tong et al., 2022) in relation to L1 and L2 reading development in future meta-analytic studies.

It would not be possible to execute the above agenda without close collaboration among a team of applied linguists, cognitive- and neuroscientists, educational psychologists, psychometricians, (teacher) educators, and policy makers.

5.3 Implications for Second Language Reading Instruction

The most important practical implication of our review and meta-analysis of metalinguistic awareness, and this Element in general, is perhaps to support teachers in developing an understanding of what metalinguistic awareness is, as well as how metalinguistic awareness functions in learning to read and reading to learn (e.g., lexical inferencing). Specifically, differentiating metalinguistic awareness from tacit linguistic knowledge (e.g., vocabulary size) to foster learning to read subskills in L2 learners will help fill the metalinguistic gap (Nagy, 2007) in classrooms composed of learners with various L1 backgrounds and L2 proficiency levels. If teachers adopt only tacit vocabulary knowledge instruction, there would be a Matthew effect, that is, learners coming to the classroom with a greater target language vocabulary size in the first place will benefit more than those bringing in a smaller vocabulary size to school, and any previously existing vocabulary gap could widen over time. Recent research has provided support for the effectiveness of metalinguistic (morphological) instruction in both L1 and L2 learners, and L2 learners may benefit more from metalinguistic instruction (e.g., Goodwin & Ahn, 2013). Metalinguistic awareness is also beneficial in promoting an analytical or words-as-tools approach in reading to learn in child or adult L2 learners (Koda & Yamashita, 2018; Nagy & Townsend, 2012).

Another notable implication is that metalinguistic instruction, in relation to reading development, should aim to foster a full metalinguistic repertoire in L2 learners instead of any single facet of metalinguistic awareness (see the Repertoire Theory of Literacy Development, Apel et al., 2004; Masterson & Apel, 2000). Convergent evidence has suggested that phonological awareness is a language-general facet of metalinguistic awareness, whereas orthographic and morphological awareness are language specific. This means that instruction in phonological awareness is less language dependent and an instruction focus on phonological/phonemic awareness can be very limited for bilingual children. Instruction in orthographic and morphological awareness should be very important and will involve more explanations of language-specific features. For example, English is morphophonemic in that the basic grapheme unit is an alphabetic letter, but printed words encode both phonemic and morphemic information, whereas Chinese orthography is morphosyllabic with the character, the basic grapheme, encoding the sound of a morpheme at the syllable level. Teachers should also (be taught to) be aware that the three facets of metalinguistic awareness play different roles from developmental and crosslinguistic perspectives. For instance, phonological awareness is an important predictor of word decoding at lower grade levels and refined morphological awareness does not surface till grade three or above in English readers. In contrast, orthographic and morphological awareness develop earlier in Chinese readers and are a more important predictor of reading comprehension in Chinese than phonological awareness. More recently, morphological awareness instruction in English has also been found to be effective and feasible for kindergartners and first- and second-grade students from low-socioeconomic-status homes (Apel & Diehm, 2014; Apel et al., 2013). A possible pathway to promote a metalinguistic repertoire in L2 learners is to promote self-teaching during reading via phonological decoding, high-quality spelling and writing, and morphological decoding and analysis, which reinforce the utilization of phonological, orthographic, and morphological awareness, respectively (e.g., Li et al., 2020).

The implications for L2 reading instruction discussed above are based on evidence reviewed in this Element as well as our understanding of the recent development in the science of reading (see the special issue *The Science of Reading: Supports, Critiques, and Questions* in *Reading Research Quarterly*, edited by Goodwin & Jiménez, 2020). Still, there is an urgent need for more collaboration between L2 reading/biliteracy researchers and teachers to conduct interventional research that verifies the causal effects of metalinguistic awareness in L2 reading, and to identify feasible and effective assessments and instructional approaches for cognitively and linguistically diverse multilingual learners.

Appendix A
Meta-Analyses and Critical Reviews Screened during the Literature Search

1. Bowers, P. N., Kirby, J. R., & Deacon, S. H. (2010). The effects of morphological instruction on literacy skills: A systematic review of the literature. *Review of Educational Research, 80*(2), 144–179.
2. Branum-Martin, L., Tao, S., & Garnaat, S. (2015). Bilingual phonological awareness: Reexamining the evidence for relations within and across languages. *Journal of Educational Psychology, 107*(1), 111–125.
3. Branum-Martin, L., Tao, S., Garnaat, S., Bunta, F., & Francis, D. J. (2012). Meta-analysis of bilingual phonological awareness: Language, age, and psycholinguistic grain size. *Journal of Educational Psychology, 104*(4), 932–944.
4. Bratlie, S. S., Brinchmann, E. I., Melby-Lervåg, M., & Torkildsen, J. V. K. (2022). Morphology – A gateway to advanced language: Meta-analysis of morphological knowledge in language-minority children. *Review of Educational Research, 92*(4), 614–650.
5. Carlisle, J. F. (2010). Effects of instruction in morphological awareness on literacy achievement: An integrative review. *Reading Research Quarterly, 45*(4), 464–487.
6. Chung, S. C., Chen, X., & Geva, E. (2019). Deconstructing and reconstructing cross-language transfer in bilingual reading development: An interactive framework. *Journal of Neurolinguistics, 50*, 149–161.
7. Goodwin, A. P., & Ahn, S. (2010). A meta-analysis of morphological interventions: Effects on literacy achievement of children with literacy difficulties. *Annals of Dyslexia, 60*(2), 183–208.
8. Goodwin, A. P., & Ahn, S. (2013). A meta-analysis of morphological interventions in English: Effects on literacy outcomes for school-age children. *Scientific Studies of Reading, 17*(4), 257–285.
9. Gottardo, A., Chen, X., & Huo, M. R. Y. (2021). Understanding within-and cross-language relations among language, preliteracy skills, and word reading in bilingual learners: Evidence from the science of reading. *Reading Research Quarterly, 56*(S1), S371–S390.
10. Hall, C., Roberts, G. J., Cho, E., McCulley, L. V., Carroll, M., & Vaughn, S. (2017). Reading instruction for English learners in the middle grades: A meta-analysis. *Educational Psychology Review, 29*(4), 763–794.

11. Jeon, E. H., & Yamashita, J. (2014). L2 reading comprehension and its correlates: A meta-analysis. *Language Learning, 64*(1), 160–212.

12. Ke, S. & Zhang, D. (2021). Morphological instruction and reading development in young L2 readers: A scoping review of causal relationships. In B. Reynolds & M. Teng (eds.), Teaching English reading and writing to young learners. Special issue of *Studies in Second Language Learning and Teaching, 11*(3), 331–350.

13. Ke, S., Miller, R. T., Zhang, D., & Koda, K. (2021). Crosslinguistic sharing of morphological awareness in biliteracy development: A systematic review and meta-analysis of correlation coefficients. *Language Learning, 71*(1), 8–54.

14. Kirby, R. J., & Bowers, P. N. (2017). Morphological instruction and literacy: Binding phonological, orthographic, and semantic features of words. In K. Cain, D. L. Compton, and R. K. Parrila, eds., *Theories of Reading Development*. Amsterdam, The Netherlands: John Benjamins, pp. 437–461.

15. Li, H., Zhang, J., & Ding, G. (2021). Reading across writing systems: A meta-analysis of the neural correlates for first and second language reading. *Bilingualism: Language and Cognition, 24*(3), 537–548.

16. Melby-Lervåg, M., & Lervåg, A. (2011). Cross-linguistic transfer of oral language, decoding, phonological awareness and reading comprehension: A meta-analysis of the correlational evidence. *Journal of Research in Reading, 34*(1), 114–135.

17. Melby-Lervåg, M., & Lervåg, A. (2014). Reading comprehension and its underlying components in second-language learners: A meta-analysis of studies comparing first- and second-language learners. *Psychological Bulletin, 140*(2), 409–433.

18. Melby-Lervåg, M., Lyster, S.-A. H., & Hulme, C. (2012). Phonological skills and their role in learning to read: A meta-analytic review. *Psychological Bulletin, 138*(2), 322–352.

19. Míguez-Álvarez, C., Cuevas-Alonso, M., & Saavedra, Á. (2021). Relationships between phonological awareness and reading in Spanish: A meta-analysis. *Language Learning, 72*(1), 113–157.

20. Nagy, W. E., Carlisle, J. F., & Goodwin, A. P. (2014). Morphological knowledge and literacy acquisition. *Journal of Learning Ddisabilities, 47*(1), 3–12.

21. Ruan, Y., Georgiou, G. K., Song, S., Li, Y., & Shu, H. (2018). Does writing system influence the associations between phonological awareness, morphological awareness, and reading? A meta-analysis. *Journal of Educational Psychology, 110*(2), 180–202.

22. Spencer, M., & Wagner, R. K. (2017). The comprehension problems for second-language learners with poor reading comprehension despite

adequate decoding: A meta-analysis. *Journal of Research in Reading,* *40*(2), 199–217.

23. Suggate, S. P. (2016). A meta-analysis of the long-term effects of phonemic awareness, phonics, fluency, and reading comprehension interventions. *Journal of Learning Disabilities, 49*(1), 77–96.

24. Yang, M., Cooc, N., & Sheng, L. (2017). An investigation of cross-linguistic transfer between Chinese and English: A meta-analysis. *Asian-Pacific Journal of Second and Foreign Language Education, 2*(1), 1–21.

Appendix B
Primary Studies Included in This Element

1. Abu-Rabia, S., & Sanitsky, E. (2010). Advantages of bilinguals over mono-linguals in learning a third language. *Bilingual Research Journal, 33*(2), 173–199.

2. Bae, H. S., & Joshi, R. (2018). A multiple-group comparison on the role of morphological awareness in reading: Within- and cross-linguistic evidence from Korean ESL and EFL learners. *Reading and Writing, 31*(8), 1821–1841.

3. Cho, J. R. (2018). Cognitive-linguistic skills and reading and writing in Korean Hangul, Chinese Hanja, and English among Korean children. In H. K. Pae, ed., *Writing Systems, Reading Processes, and Cross-Linguistic Influences: Reflections from the Chinese, Japanese and Korean Languages.* Amsterdam; Philadelphia: John Benjamins, pp. 391–410.

4. Chung, K. K. H., & Ho, C. S. H. (2010). Second language learning difficul-ties in Chinese children with dyslexia: What are the reading-related cognitive skills that contribute to English and Chinese word reading? *Journal of Learning Disabilities, 43*(3), 195–211.

5. Deacon, S. H., Wade-Woolley, L., & Kirby, J. R. (2009). Flexibility in young second-language learners: Examining the language specificity of orthographic processing. *Journal of Research in Reading, 32*(2), 215–229.

6. Lo, J. C. M., Ye, Y., Tong, X., McBride, C., Ho, C. S. H., & Waye, M. M. Y. (2018). Delayed copying is uniquely related to dictation in bilingual Cantonese–English-speaking children in Hong Kong. *Writing Systems Research, 10*(1), 26–42.

7. Luo, Y. (2013). Biliteracy development in Chinese and English: The roles of phonological awareness, morphological awareness and orthographic pro-cessing in word-level reading and vocabulary acquisition. Unpublished doctoral dissertation, University of Toronto.

8. Russak, S. (2020). The contribution of cognitive and linguistic skills in L1 and EFL to English spelling among native speakers of Arabic and Hebrew. *Cognitive Development, 55*, 100924.

9. Tong, X., & McBride-Chang, C. (2010). Chinese-English biscriptal reading: Cognitive component skills across orthographies. *Reading and Writing, 23*(3), 293–310.

10. Wang, M., Lin, C. Y., & Yang, C. (2014). Contributions of phonology, orthography, and morphology in Chinese-English biliteracy acquisition: A one-year longitudinal study. In X. Chen, Q. Wang, and Y.C. Luo, eds., *Reading Development and Difficulties in Monolingual and Bilingual Chinese Children*. Dordrecht: Springer, pp. 191–211.

11. Wang, M., Yang, C., & Cheng, C. (2009). The contributions of phonology, orthography, and morphology in Chinese–English biliteracy acquisition. *Applied Psycholinguistics*, *30*(2), 291–314.

12. Wong, Y. K., & Zhou, Y. (2021). Effects of metalinguistic awareness on Chinese as a second language spelling through the mediation of reading and copying. *Reading and Writing*, *35*, 853–875.

13. Zhang, D. (2017a). Multidimensionality of morphological awareness and text comprehension among young Chinese readers in a multilingual context. *Learning and Individual Differences*, *56*, 13–23.

14. Zhang, D. (2017b). Word reading in L1 and L2 learners of Chinese: Similarities and differences in the functioning of component processes. *The Modern Language Journal*, *101*(2), 391–411.

15. Zhao, J., Joshi, R. M., Dixon, L. Q., & Chen, S. (2017). Contribution of phonological, morphological and orthographic awareness to English word spelling: A comparison of EL1 and EFL models. *Contemporary Educational Psychology*, *49*, 185–194.

16. Zhou, Y., McBride, C., Leung, J. S. M., Wang, Y., Joshi, M., & Farver, J. (2018). Chinese and English reading-related skills in L1 and L2 Chinese-speaking children in Hong Kong. *Language, Cognition and Neuroscience*, *33*(3), 300–312.

References

Abu-Rabia, S. (2001). Testing the interdependence hypothesis among native adult bilingual Russian–English students. *Journal of Psycholinguistic Research*, *30*, 437–455.

Abu-Rabia, S., & Sanitsky, E. (2010). Advantages of bilinguals over monolinguals in learning a third language. *Bilingual Research Journal*, *33*(2), 173–199.

Alderson, J. C. (1984). Reading in a foreign language: A reading problem or a language problem? In J. C. Alderson & A. H. Urquhart, eds., *Reading in a Foreign Language*. London: Longman, pp. 1–24.

Apel, K. (2011). What is orthographic knowledge? *Language, Speech, and Hearing Services in Schools*, *42*(4), 592–603.

Apel, K., & Diehm, E. (2014). Morphological awareness intervention with kindergarteners and first and second grade students from low SES homes: A small efficacy study. *Journal of Learning Disabilities*, *47*(1), 65–75.

Apel, K., Brimo, D., Diehm, E., & Apel, L. (2013). Morphological awareness intervention with kindergartners and first- and second-grade students from low socioeconomic status homes: A feasibility study. *Journal of Learning Disabilities*, *47*(1), 65–75.

Apel, K., Henbest, V. S., & Masterson, J. (2019). Orthographic knowledge: Clarifications, challenges, and future directions. *Reading and Writing*, *32*(4), 873–889.

Apel, K., Masterson, J., & Hart, P. (2004). Integration of language components in spelling: Instructions that maximize students' learning. In E. R. Silliman & L. C. Wilkinson, eds., *Language and Literacy Learning in Schools*. New York: Guilford, pp. 292–318.

Apel, K., Wilson-Fowler, E. B., Brimo, D., & Perrin, N. A. (2012). Metalinguistic contributions to reading and spelling in second and third grade students. *Reading and Writing*, *25*(6), 1283–1305.

Badian, N. A. (2001). Phonological and orthographic processing: Their roles in reading prediction. *Annals of Dyslexia*, *51*(1), 177–202.

Bae, H. S., & Joshi, R. (2018). A multiple-group comparison on the role of morphological awareness in reading: Within- and cross-linguistic evidence from Korean ESL and EFL learners. *Reading and Writing*, *31*(8), 1821–1841.

Bernhardt, E., & Kamil, M. (1995). Interpreting relationships between L1 and L2 reading: Consolidating the linguistic threshold and the linguistic interdependence hypotheses. *Applied Linguistics*, *16*(1), 15–34.

Berninger, V. (1994). Introduction to the varieties of orthographic knowledge I: Theoretical and developmental issues. In V. W. Berninger, ed., *The Varieties of Orthographic Knowledge*. Dordrecht: Springer, pp. 1–25.

Berninger, V., & Nagy, W. (1999). University of Washington morphological awareness battery. Unpublished experimental test battery, Seattle, WA.

Bernstein, S. E., Flipse, J. L., Jin, Y., & Odegard, T. N. (2020). Word and sentence level tests of morphological awareness in reading. *Reading and Writing, 33*(6), 1591–1616.

Bialystok, E. (2001). Metalinguistic aspects of bilingual processing. *Annual Review of Applied Linguistics, 21*, 169–181.

Bialystok, E., & Ryan, E. B. (1985). Toward a definition of metalinguistic skill. *Merrill-Palmer Quarterly, 31*(3), 229–251.

Borenstein, M., Hedges, L. V., Higgins, J. P. T., & Rothstein, H. R. (2009). *Introduction to Meta-Analysis*. Chichester, UK: Wiley.

Borenstein, M., Hedges, L., & Rothstein, H. (2007). Meta-analysis: Fixed effect vs random effects. www.meta-analysis.com/downloads/M-a_f_e_v_r_e_sv .pdf

Branum-Martin, L., Tao, S., Garnaat, S., Bunta, F., & Francis, D. J. (2012). Meta-analysis of bilingual phonological awareness: Language, age, and psycholinguistic grain size. *Journal of Educational Psychology, 104*(4), 932–944.

Bratlie, S. S., Brinchmann, E. I., Melby-Lervåg, M., & Torkildsen, J. V. K. (2022). Morphology – A gateway to advanced language: Meta-analysis of morphological knowledge in language-minority children. *Review of Educational Research, 92*(4), 614–650.

Brimo, D., Apel, K., & Fountain, T. (2017). Examining the contributions of syntactic awareness and syntactic knowledge to reading comprehension. *Journal of Research in Reading, 40*(1), 57–74.

Cain, K. (2007). Syntactic awareness and reading ability: Is there any evidence for a special relationship? *Applied Psycholinguistics, 28*(4), 679–694.

Carlisle, J. F. (1995). Morphological awareness and early reading achievement. In L. B. Feldman, ed., *Morphological Aspects of Language Processing*. Hillsdale, NJ: Lawrence Erlbaum, pp. 189–209.

Carlisle, J. F. (2000). Awareness of the structure and meaning of morphologically complex words: Impact on reading. *Reading and Writing, 12*, 169–190.

Carrell, P. L. (1991). Second language reading: Reading ability or language proficiency? *Applied Linguistics, 12*(2), 159–179.

Chen, T., Ke, S., & Koda, K. (2021). The predictive role of early graphomorphological knowledge in later reading comprehension in L2 Chinese. *Frontiers in Psychology*, 4870. https://doi.org/10.3389/fpsyg.2021.757934

Cheung, M. W. L. (2014). Fixed- and random-effects meta-analytic structural equation modeling: Examples and analyses in R. *Behavior Research Methods*, *46*(1), 29–40.

Cheung, M. W. L., & Chan, W. (2005). Meta-analytic structural equation modeling: A two-stage approach. *Psychological Methods*, *10*(1), 40–64.

Chung, S. C., Chen, X., & Deacon, S. H. (2018). The relation between orthographic processing and spelling in grade 1 French immersion children. *Journal of Research in Reading*, *41*(2), 290–311.

Chung, S. C., Chen, X., & Geva, E. (2019). Deconstructing and reconstructing cross-language transfer in bilingual reading development: An interactive framework. *Journal of Neurolinguistics*, *50*, 149–161.

Clarke, M. A. (1980). The short circuit hypothesis of ESL reading – or when language competence interferes with reading performance. *The Modern Language Journal*, *64*(2), 203–209.

Commissaire, E., Duncan, L. G., & Casalis, S. (2011). Cross-language transfer of orthographic processing skills: A study of French children who learn English at school. *Journal of Research in Reading*, *34*(1),59–76.

Cuijpers, P., Griffin, J., & Furukawa, T. (2021). The lack of statistical power of subgroup analyses in meta-analyses: A cautionary note. *Epidemiology and Psychiatric Sciences*, *30*, E78. https://doi.org/10.1017/S2045796021000664

Cummins, J. (1979). Linguistic interdependence and the educational development of bilingual children. *Review of Educational Research*, *49*(2), 222–251.

Cummins, J. (1981). The role of primary language development in promoting educational success for language minority students. In California State Department of Education, ed., *Schooling and Language Minority Students: A Theoretical Framework*. Los Angeles, CA: Evaluation, Dissemination and Assessment Center, California State University, pp. 3–49.

Deacon, S. H., Kieffer, M. J., & Laroche, A. (2014). The relation between morphological awareness and reading comprehension: Evidence from mediation and longitudinal models. *Scientific Studies of Reading*, *18*(6), 432–451.

Deacon, S. H., Wade-Woolley, L., & Kirby, J. R. (2009). Flexibility in young second-language learners: Examining the language specificity of orthographic processing. *Journal of Research in Reading*, *32*(2), 215–229.

Ehri, L. C. (2005). Development of sight word reading: Phases and findings. In M. J. Snowling & C. Hulme, eds., *The Science of Reading: A Handbook*. Malden, MA: Blackwell, pp. 135–154.

Elleman, A. M., Lindo, E. J., Morphy, P., & Compton, D. L. (2009). The impact of vocabulary instruction on passage-level comprehension of school-age children: A meta-analysis. *Journal of Research on Educational Effectiveness*, *2*(1), 1–44.

Eviatar, Z., Taha, H., & Shwartz, M. (2018). Metalinguistic awareness and literacy among semitic-bilingual learners: A cross-language perspective. *Reading and Writing, 31*, 1869–1891.

Genesee, F., Geva, E., Dressler, C., & Kamil, M. (2006). Synthesis: Cross-linguistic relationships in working memory, phonological processes, and oral language. In D. August & T. Shanahan, eds., *Developing Literacy in Second-Language Learners: Report of the National Literacy Panel on Language-Minority Children and Youth*. Mahwah, NJ: Lawrence Erlbaum, pp. 153–174.

Georgiou, G. K., Martinez, D., Vieira, A. P. A., & Guo, K. (2021). Is orthographic knowledge a strength or a weakness in individuals with dyslexia? Evidence from a meta-analysis. *Annals of Dyslexia, 71*(1), 5–27.

Geva, E., & Ryan, E. B. (1993). Linguistic and cognitive correlates of academic skills in first and second language. *Language Learning, 43*, 5–42.

Geva, E., & Siegel, L. S. (2000). Orthographic and cognitive factors in the concurrent development of basic reading skills in two languages. *Reading and Writing, 12*(1), 1–30.

Gombert, J. (1992). *Metalinguistic Development*. Chicago: University of Chicago University Press.

Goodwin, A. P., & Ahn, S. (2010). A meta-analysis of morphological interventions: Effects on literacy achievement of children with literacy difficulties. *Annals of Dyslexia, 60*(2), 183–208.

Goodwin, A. P., & Ahn, S. (2013). A meta-analysis of morphological interventions in English: Effects on literacy outcomes for school-age children. *Scientific Studies of Reading, 17*(4), 257–285.

Goodwin, A., & Jiménez, R. T. (2020). The science of reading: Supports, critiques, and questions. *Reading Research Quarterly, 55*(S1), S7–S16.

Goswami, U., & Bryant, P. (1990). *Phonological Skills and Learning to Read*. Hillsdale, NJ: Erlbaum.

Gottardo, A., Chen, X., & Huo, M. R. Y. (2021). Understanding within-and cross-language relations among language, preliteracy skills, and word reading in bilingual learners: Evidence from the science of reading. *Reading Research Quarterly, 56*(S1), S371–S390.

Gottardo, A., Yan, B., Siegel, L. S., & Wade–Woolley, L. (2001). Factors related to English reading performance in children with Chinese as a first language: More evidence of cross language transfer of phonological processing. *Journal of Educational Psychology, 93*(3), 530–542.

Haastrup, K. (1991). *Lexical Inferencing Procedures, or, Talking About Words: Receptive Procedures in Foreign Language Learning with Special Reference to English*. Tubingen, Germany: Gunter Narr Verlag.

Halliday, M. A. K. (1981). The origin and early development of Chinese phonological theory. In R. E. Asher & E.J. A. Henderson, eds., *Towards a Theory of Phonetics*. Edinburgh: Edinburgh University Press, pp. 123–140.

Hatakeyama, M. (2012). Lexical inferencing in L2 Japanese reading: L2 proficiency and L1 reading as predictors of semantic gap filling (SGF) at word level. *J-Stage*, *9*, 13–31.

Hedges, L. V., & Olkin, I. (1985). *Statistical Methods for Meta-Analysis*. Orlando, FL: Academic Press.

Hohn, R. E., Slaney, K. L., & Tafreshi, D. (2019). Primary study quality in psychological meta-analyses: An empirical assessment of recent practice. *Frontiers in Psychology*, *9*, 2667.

Hu, M., & Nation, I. S.P. (2000). Unknown vocabulary density and reading comprehension. *Reading in a Foreign Language*, *13*(1), 403–430.

Jak, S., & Cheung, M. W. L. (2020). Meta-analytic structural equation modeling with moderating effects on SEM parameters. *Psychological Methods*, *25*(4), 430–455.

Jeon, E. H., & Yamashita, J. (2014). L2 reading comprehension and its correlates: A meta-analysis. *Language Learning*, *64*(1), 160–212.

Kang, J. Y. (2013). Decontextualized language production in two languages: An investigation of children's word definition skills in Korean and English. *Applied Psycholinguistics*, *34*(2), 211–231.

Ke, S., & Koda, K. (2017). Contributions of morphological awareness to adult L2 Chinese word meaning inferencing. *The Modern Language Journal*, *101*(4), 742–755.

Ke, S., & Koda, K. (2019). Is vocabulary knowledge sufficient for word meaning inference? An investigation of the role of morphological awareness in adult L2 learners of Chinese. *Applied Linguistics*, *40*(3), 456–477.

Ke, S., Miller, R., Zhang, D., & Koda, K. (2021). Crosslinguistic sharing of morphological awareness in biliteracy development: A systematic review and meta-analysis of correlation coefficients. *Language Learning*, *71*(1), 8–54.

Ke, S., & Koda, K. (2021). Transfer facilitation effects of morphological awareness on multicharacter word reading in Chinese as a second language. *Applied Psycholinguistics*, *42*(5), 1263–1286.

Ke, S., & Zhang, D. (2021). Morphological instruction and reading development in young L2 readers: A scoping review of causal relationships. In B. Reynolds & M. Teng, eds., Teaching English reading and writing to young learners. Special issue of *Studies in Second Language Learning and Teaching*, *11*(3), 331–350.

Kerlinger, F. N. (1999). *Foundations of Behavioral Research*. New York: Wadsworth.

Kieffer, M. J., Biancarosa, G., & Mancilla-Martinez, J. (2013). Roles of morphological awareness in the reading comprehension of Spanish-speaking language minority learners: Exploring partial mediation by vocabulary and reading fluency. *Applied Psycholinguistics, 34*(4), 697–725.

Kirby, R. J., & Bowers, P. N. (2017). Morphological instruction and literacy: Binding phonological, orthographic, and semantic features of words. In K. Cain, D. L. Compton, and R. K. Parrila, eds., *Theories of Reading Development*. Amsterdam, The Netherlands: John Benjamins, pp. 437–461.

Koda, K. (2005). *Insights into Second Language Reading: A Cross-Linguistic Approach*. New York: Cambridge University Press.

Koda, K. (2007). Reading and language learning: Cross-linguistic constraints on second language reading development. *Language Learning, 57*(Suppl.1), 1–44.

Koda, K. (2008). Impacts of prior literacy experience on second-language learning to read. In K. Koda & A. M. Zehler, eds., *Learning to Read Across Languages: Cross-Linguistic Relationships in First- and Second-Language Literacy Development*. New York: Routledge, pp. 68–96.

Koda, K., & Ke, S. (2018). L1-induced facilitation in L2 reading development (in Chinese). *Journal of International Chinese Teaching, 18*(2), 40–48.

Koda, K., Lü, C., & Zhang, D. (2014). L1-induced facilitation in biliteracy development in Chinese and English. In X. Chen, Q. Wang, & Y. Luo, eds., *Reading Development and Difficulties in Monolingual and Bilingual Chinese Children*. New York: Springer, pp. 141–170.

Koda, K., & Miller, R. T. (2018). Cross-linguistic interaction in L2 word meaning inference in English as a foreign language. In H. K. Pae, ed., *Writing Systems, Reading Processes, and Cross-Linguistic Influences: Reflections from the Chinese, Japanese and Korean Languages*. Philadelphia, PA: John Benjamins, pp. 293–312.

Koda, K., & Reddy, P. (2008). Cross-linguistic transfer in second language reading. *Language Teaching, 41*(4), 497–508.

Koda, K., & Yamashita, J. (2018). *Reading to Learn in a Foreign Language: An Integrated Approach to Foreign Language Instruction and Assessment*. New York: Routledge.

Kuo, L. J., & Anderson, R. C. (2008). Conceptual and methodological issues in comparing metalinguistic awareness across languages. In K. Koda & A. M. Zehler, eds., *Learning to Read Across Languages: Cross-Linguistic Relationships in First- and Second-Language Literacy Development*. New York: Routledge, pp. 39–67.

Kuo, L. J., & Anderson, R. C. (2010). Beyond cross-language transfer: Reconceptualizing the impact of early bilingualism on phonological awareness. *Scientific Studies of Reading, 14*(4), 365–385.

Lado, R. (1957). *Linguistics Across Cultures: Applied Linguistics for Language Teachers*. Ann Arbor, MI: University of Michigan Press.

Leong, C. K., Tse, S. K., Loh, K. Y., & Ki, W. W. (2011). Orthographic knowledge important in comprehending elementary Chinese text by users of alphasyllabaries. *Reading Psychology, 32*(3), 237–271.

Levesque, K. C., Breadmore, H. L., & Deacon, S. H. (2021). How morphology impacts reading and spelling: Advancing the role of morphology in models of literacy development. *Journal of Research in Reading, 44*(1), 10–26.

Li, L., & Wu, X. (2015). Effects of metalinguistic awareness on reading comprehension and the mediator role of reading fluency from grades 2 to 4. *PLOS ONE, 10*(3), e0114417.

Li, X., & Koda, K. (2022). Linguistic constraints on the cross-linguistic variations in L2 word recognition. *Reading and Writing, 35*, 1401–1424.

Li, Y. (2021). How do children learn new words in a second language? The role of self-teaching in orthographic learning. Unpublished doctoral dissertation, University of Maryland.

Li, Y., Li, H., & Wang, M. (2020). The roles of phonological recoding, semantic radicals and writing practice in orthographic learning in Chinese. *Scientific Studies of Reading, 24*(3), 252–263.

Liu, N., & Nation, P. (1985). Factors affecting guessing vocabulary in context. *RECL Journal, 16*(1), 33–42.

Luo, Y. (2013). Biliteracy development in Chinese and English: The roles of phonological awareness, morphological awareness and orthographic processing in word-level reading and vocabulary acquisition. Unpublished doctoral dissertation, University of Toronto.

Marsden, E., Morgan-Short, K., Thompson, S., & Abugaber, D. (2018). Replication in second language research: Narrative and systematic reviews and recommendations for the field. *Language Learning, 68*(2), 321–391.

Masterson, J. J., & Apel, K. (2000). Spelling assessment: Charting a path to optimal intervention. *Topics in Language Disorders, 20*(3), 50–65.

McBride-Chang, C. (1995). What is phonological awareness? *Journal of Educational Psychology, 87*(2), 179–192.

McBride-Chang, C., Cho, J. R., Liu, H., Wagner, R. K., Shu, H., Zhou, A., Cheuk, C. S., & Muse, A. (2005). Changing models across cultures: Associations of phonological awareness and morphological structure awareness with vocabulary and word recognition in second graders from Beijing,

Hong Kong, Korea, and the United States. *Journal of Experimental Child Psychology, 92*(2), 140–160.

McBride-Chang, C., Tardif, T., Cho, J. R., Shu, H. U. A., Fletcher, P., Stokes, S. F., Wong, A., & Leung, K. (2008). What's in a word? Morphological awareness and vocabulary knowledge in three languages. *Applied Psycholinguistics, 29*(3), 437–462.

McBride-Chang, C., Wagner, R. K., Muse, A., Chow, B. W. Y., & Shu, H. U. A. (2005). The role of morphological awareness in children's vocabulary acquisition in English. *Applied Psycholinguistics, 26*(3), 415–435.

Meara, P. (1996). The dimensions of lexical competence. In G. Brown, K. Malmkjaer, and J. Williams, eds., *Performance and Competence in Second Language Acquisition*. Cambridge, UK: Cambridge University Press, pp. 33–55.

Melby-Lervåg, M., & Lervåg, A. (2011). Cross-linguistic transfer of oral language, decoding, phonological awareness and reading comprehension: A meta-analysis of the correlational evidence. *Journal of Research in Reading, 34*(1), 114–135.

Messick, S. (1989). Validity. In R. L. Linn (Ed.), *Educational Measurement*, 3rd ed. New York: American Council on Education, pp. 13–103.

Míguez-Álvarez, C., Cuevas-Alonso, M., & Saavedra, Á. (2021). Relationships between phonological awareness and reading in Spanish: A meta-analysis. *Language Learning, 72*(1), 113–157.

Nagy, W. (2007). Metalinguistic awareness and the vocabulary-comprehension connection. In R. K. Wagner, A. E. Muse, and K. R. Tannenbaum, eds., *Vocabulary Acquisition: Implications for Reading Comprehension*. London; New York: Guilford Press, pp. 52–77.

Nagy, W. E., & Anderson, R. C. (1995). *Metalinguistic Awareness and Literacy Acquisition in Different Languages*. Center for the Study of Reading technical report no. 618. Urbana, IL: Center for the Study of Reading.

Nagy, W., Berninger, V., Abbott, R., Vaughan, K., & Vermeulen, K. (2003). Relationship of morphology and other language skills to literacy skills in at-risk second-grade readers and at-risk fourth-grade writers. *Journal of Educational Psychology, 95*(4), 730–742.

Nagy, W. E., Carlisle, J. F., & Goodwin, A. P. (2014). Morphological knowledge and literacy acquisition. *Journal of Learning Disabilities, 47*(1), 3–12.

Nagy, W., & Townsend, D. (2012). Words as tools: Learning academic vocabulary as language acquisition. *Reading Research Quarterly, 47*(1), 91–108.

Nassaji, H. (2003). L2 vocabulary learning from context: Strategies, knowledge sources, and their relationship with success in L2 lexical inferencing. *TESOL Quarterly, 37*(4), 645–670.

Nassaji, H. (2006). The relationship between depth of vocabulary knowledge and L2 learners' lexical inferencing strategy use and success. *The Modern Language Journal, 90*(3), 387–401.

Nassaji, H., & Geva, E. (1999). The contribution of phonological and orthographic processing skills to adult ESL reading: Evidence from native speakers of Farsi. *Applied Psycholinguistics, 20*(2), 241–267.

Nation, I. S. P. (2001). *Learning Vocabulary in Another Language.* Cambridge: Cambridge University Press.

Nation, I. (2006). How large a vocabulary is needed for reading and listening? *Canadian Modern Language Review, 63*(1), 59–82.

Nunes, T., Bryant, P., & Bindman, M. (1997). Morphological spelling strategies: Developmental stages and processes. *Developmental Psychology, 33*(4), 637–649.

Ordóñez, C. L., Carlo, M. S., Snow, C. E., & McLaughlin, B. (2002). Depth and breadth of vocabulary in two languages: Which vocabulary skills transfer? *Journal of Educational Psychology, 94*(4), 719–728.

Pan, J., Song, S., Su, M., McBride, C., Liu, H., Zhang, Y., . . . & Shu, H. (2016). On the relationship between phonological awareness, morphological awareness and Chinese literacy skills: Evidence from an 8-year longitudinal study. *Developmental Science, 19*(6), 982–991.

Paribakht, T. S., & Wesche, M. (1999). "Incidental" vocabulary acquisition through reading: An introspective study. *Studies in Second Language Acquisition, 21*(2), 203–220.

Pasquarella, A., Deacon, H., Chen, X., Commissaire, & Au-Yeung, K. (2014). Acquiring orthographic processing through word reading: Evidence from children learning to read French and English. *International Journal of Disability, Development and Education, 61*(3), 240–257.

Peng, P., Lee, K., Luo, J., Li, S., Joshi, R. M., & Tao, S. (2021). Simple view of reading in Chinese: A one-stage meta-analytic structural equation modeling. *Review of Educational Research, 91*(1), 3–33.

Perfetti, C. A. (2003). The universal grammar of reading. *Scientific Studies of Reading, 7*(1), 3–24.

Perfetti, C. A. (2007). Reading ability: Lexical quality to comprehension. *Scientific Studies of Reading, 11*(4), 357–383.

Perfetti, C. A., & Hart, L. (2002). The lexical quality hypothesis. In L. Vehoeven, C. Elbro, & P. Reitsma, eds., *Precursors of Functional Literacy.* Amsterdam: John Benjamins, pp. 189–213.

Perfetti, C., & Stafura, J. (2014). Word knowledge in a theory of reading comprehension. *Scientific Studies of Reading, 18*(1), 22–37.

Plaut, D. C., McClelland, J. L., Seidenberg, M. S., & Patterson, K. (1996). Understanding normal and impaired word reading: Computational principles in quasi-regular domains. *Psychological Review, 103*(1), 56–115.

Plonsky, L., & Derrick, D. J. (2016). A meta-analysis of reliability coefficients in second language research. *The Modern Language Journal, 100*(2), 538–553.

Plonsky, L., & Ghanbar, H. (2018). Multiple regression in L2 research: A methodological synthesis and guide to interpreting R2 values. *The Modern Language Journal, 102*(4), 713–731.

Plonsky, L., & Oswald, F. L. (2014). How big is "big"? Interpreting effect sizes in L2 research. *Language Learning, 64*(4), 878–912.

Qian, D. D. (1998). Depth of vocabulary knowledge: Assessing its role in adults' reading comprehension in English as a Second Language. Unpublished doctoral dissertation, University of Toronto.

Qian, D. D. (2005). Demystifying lexical inferencing: The role of aspects of vocabulary knowledge. *TESL Canada Journal, 22*(2), 34–54.

Read, J. (1993). The development of a new measure of L2 vocabulary knowledge. *Language Testing, 10*(3), 355–371.

Read, J. (2000). *Assessing Vocabulary.* Cambridge, UK: Cambridge University Press.

Reddy, P. P., & Koda, K. (2013). Orthographic constraints on phonological awareness in biliteracy development. *Writing Systems Research, 5*(1), 110–130.

Riches, C., & Genesee, F. (2006). Crosslanguage and crossmodal influences. In F. Genesee, K. Lindholm-Leary, W. Saunders, and D. Christian, eds., *Educating English Language Learners: A Synthesis of Research Evidence.* New York: Cambridge University Press, pp. 64–87.

Ricketts, J., Bishop, D. V., & Nation, K. (2009). Orthographic facilitation in oral vocabulary acquisition. *Quarterly Journal of Experimental Psychology, 62*(10), 1948–1966.

Roehr-Brackin, K. (2018). *Metalinguistic Awareness and Second Language Acquisition.* New York: Routledge.

Ruan, Y., Georgiou, G. K., Song, S., Li, Y., & Shu, H. (2018). Does writing system influence the associations between phonological awareness, morphological awareness, and reading? A meta-analysis. *Journal of Educational Psychology, 110*(2), 180–202.

Russak, S. (2020). The contribution of cognitive and linguistic skills in L1 and EFL to English spelling among native speakers of Arabic and Hebrew. *Cognitive Development, 55*, 100924.

Saiegh-Haddad, E., & Geva, E. (2008). Morphological awareness, phonological awareness, and reading in English–Arabic bilingual children. *Reading and Writing, 21*, 481–504.

Saiegh-Haddad, E., Lask, L., & McBride, C. (eds.). (2022). *Handbook of Literacy in Diglossia and in Dialectal Contexts: Psycholinguistic, Neurolinguistic, and Educational Perspectives*. Springer.

Salins, A., Cupples, L., Leigh, G., & Castles, A. (2022). Orthographic facilitation of oral vocabulary acquisition in primary school children. *Quarterly Journal of Experimental Psychology*. https://doi.org/10.1177/17470218221102916

Schatschneider, C., Francis, D. J., Foorman, B. R., Fletcher, J. M., & Mehta, P. (1999). The dimensionality of phonological awareness: An application of item response theory. *Journal of Educational Psychology, 91*(3), 439–449.

Schmitt, N., Jiang, X., & Grabe, W. (2011). The percentage of words known in a text and reading comprehension. *The Modern Language Journal, 95*(1), 26–43.

Seidenberg, M. S., & McClelland, J. L. (1989). A distributed, developmental model of word recognition and naming. *Psychological Review, 96*(4), 523–568.

Share, D. L. (2021). Is the science of reading just the science of reading English? *Reading Research Quarterly, 56*(S1), S391–S402.

Singson, M., Mahony, D., & Mann, V. (2000). The relation between reading ability and morphological skills: Evidence from derivational suffixes. *Reading and Writing, 12*, 219–252.

Sohail, J., Sorenson Duncan, T., Koh, P. W., Deacon, S. H., & Chen, X. (2022). How syntactic awareness might influence reading comprehension in English–French bilingual children. *Reading and Writing, 35*(5), 1289–1313.

Sparks, R. L., & Ganschow, L. (1991). Foreign language learning differences: Affective or native language aptitude differences? *The Modern Language Journal, 75*(1), 3–16.

Sparks, R., Ganschow, L., & Pohlman, J. (1989). Linguistic coding deficits in foreign language learners. *Annals of Dyslexia, 39*(1), 177–195.

Stahl, S. A., & Murray, B. A. (1994). Defining phonological awareness and its relationship to early reading. *Journal of Educational Psychology, 86*(2), 221–234.

Sun-Alperin, M. K., & Wang, M. (2011). Cross-language transfer of phonological and orthographic processing skills from Spanish L1 to English L2. *Reading and Writing, 24*, 591–614.

Templeton, S., & Morris, D. (2000). Spelling. In M. Kamil, P. Mosenthal, P. D. Pearson, & R. Barr, eds., *Handbook of Reading Research*. Mahwah, NJ: Erlbaum, pp. 525–543.

Tighe, E. L., Little, C. W., Arrastia-Chisholm, M. C., Schatschneider, C., Diehm, E., Quinn, J. M., & Edwards, A. A. (2019). Assessing the direct and indirect effects of metalinguistic awareness to the reading comprehension skills of struggling adult readers. *Reading and Writing, 32*(3), 787–818.

Tong, X., Kwan, J. L. Y., Tong, S., & Deacon, S. H. (2022). How Chinese–English bilingual fourth graders draw on syntactic awareness in reading comprehension: Within-and cross-language effects. *Reading Research Quarterly, 57*(2), 409–429.

Tunmer, W. E., Pratt, C., & Herriman, M. L. (1984.). *Metalinguistic Awareness in Children: Theory, Research, and Implications.* New York: Springer-Verlag.

Valentine, J. C., Pigott, T. D., & Rothstein, H. R. (2010). How many studies do you need? A primer on statistical power for meta-analysis. *Journal of Educational and Behavioral Statistics, 35*(2), 215–247.

Wagner, R. K., & Meros, D. (2010). Vocabulary and reading comprehension: Direct, indirect, and reciprocal influences. *Focus on Exceptional Children,* 1G1-245473138.

Wang, M., Lin, C. Y., & Yang, C. (2014). Contributions of phonology, orthography, and morphology in Chinese–English biliteracy acquisition: A one-year longitudinal study. In X. Chen Q. Wang, and Y.C. Luo, eds., *Reading Development and Difficulties in Monolingual and Bilingual Chinese Children.* Dordrecht: Springer, pp. 191–211.

Wang, M., Yang, C., & Cheng, C. (2009). The contributions of phonology, orthography, and morphology in Chinese–English biliteracy acquisition. *Applied Psycholinguistics, 30*(2), 291–314.

Williams, J. P., & Atkins, J. G. (2009). The role of metacognition in teaching reading comprehension to primary students. In D. J. Hacker, J. Dunlosky, & A. C. Graesser, eds., *Handbook of Metacognition in Education.* New York: Routledge, pp. 26–43.

Wong, Y. K., & Zhou, Y. (2021). Effects of metalinguistic awareness on Chinese as a second language spelling through the mediation of reading and copying. *Reading and Writing, 35,* 853–875.

Yuill, N. (2007). Visiting joke city: How can talking about jokes foster metalinguistic awareness in poor comprehenders In D. McNamara, ed., *Reading Comprehension Strategies: Theories, Interventions, and Technologies.* London: Routledge, pp. 325–345.

Zhang, D. (2016). Morphology in Malay–English biliteracy acquisition: An intervention study. *International Journal of Bilingual Education and Bilingualism, 19*(5), 546–562.

Zhang, D. (2017a). Multidimensionality of morphological awareness and text comprehension among young Chinese readers in a multilingual context. *Learning and Individual Differences, 56,* 13–23.

Zhang, D. (2017b). Word reading in L1 and L2 learners of Chinese: Similarities and differences in the functioning of component processes. *The Modern Language Journal, 101*(2), 391–411.

Zhang, D., & Ke, S. (2019). The simple view of reading made complex by morphological decoding fluency in bilingual fourth-grade readers of English. *Reading Research Quarterly, 55*(2), 311–329.

Zhang, D., & Koda, K. (2012). Contribution of morphological awareness and lexical inferencing ability to L2 vocabulary knowledge and reading comprehension among advanced EFL learners: Testing direct and indirect effects. *Reading and Writing, 25*(5), 1195–1216.

Zhang, D., & Koda, K. (2013). Morphological awareness and reading comprehension in a foreign language: A study of young Chinese EFL learners. *System, 41*(4), 901–913.

Zhang, D., & Yang, X. (2016). Chinese L2 learners' depth of vocabulary knowledge and its role in reading comprehension. *Foreign Language Annals, 49*(4), 699–715.

Zhang, H., & Koda, K. (2018). Vocabulary knowledge and morphological awareness in Chinese as a heritage language (CHL) reading comprehension ability. *Reading and Writing, 31*, 53–74.

Zhang, H., & Koda, K. (2021). Cross-linguistic morphological awareness in Chinese heritage language reading acquisition. *Journal of Psycholinguistic Research, 50*(2), 335–353.

Zhang, H., & Lin, J. (2021). Morphological knowledge in second language reading comprehension: Examining mediation through vocabulary knowledge and lexical inference. *Educational Psychology, 41*(5), 563–581.

Zhang, J., Lin, T. J., Liu, Y., & Nagy, W. E. (2020). Morphological awareness and reading comprehension: Differential mediation mechanisms in native English speakers, fluent English learners, and limited English learners. *Journal of Experimental Child Psychology, 199*, 104915.

Zhao, J., Joshi, R. M., Dixon, L. Q., & Chen, S. (2017). Contribution of phonological, morphological and orthographic awareness to English word spelling: A comparison of EL1 and EFL models. *Contemporary Educational Psychology, 49*, 185–194.

Zhao, Y., Wu, X., Sun, P., Xie, R., Feng, J., & Chen, H. (2019). The relationship between morphological awareness and reading comprehension among Chinese children: Evidence from multiple mediation models. *Learning and Individual Differences, 72*, 59–68.

Zhou, Y., McBride, C., Leung, J. S. M., Wang, Y., Joshi, M., & Farver, J. (2018). Chinese and English reading-related skills in L1 and L2 Chinese-speaking children in Hong Kong. *Language, Cognition and Neuroscience, 33*(3), 300–312.

Ziegler, J. C., & Goswami, U. (2005). Reading acquisition, developmental dyslexia, and skilled reading across languages: A psycholinguistic grain size theory. *Psychological Bulletin, 131*(1), 3–29.

Ziegler, J. C., & Goswami, U. (2006). Becoming literate in different languages: Similar problems, different solutions. *Developmental Science, 9*(5), 429–436.

Zipke, M., Ehri, L. C., & Cairns, H. S. (2009). Using semantic ambiguity instruction to improve third graders' metalinguistic awareness and reading comprehension: An experimental study. *Reading Research Quarterly, 44*(3), 300–321.

Cambridge Elements ☰

Applied Linguistics

Li Wei
University College London

Li Wei is Chair of Applied Linguistics at the UCL Institute of Education, University College London (UCL), and Fellow of the Academy of Social Sciences, UK. His research covers different aspects of bilingualism and multilingualism. He was the founding editor of the following journals: *International Journal of Bilingualism* (SAGE), *Applied Linguistics Review* (De Gruyter), *Language, Culture and Society* (Benjamins), *Chinese Language and Discourse* (Benjamins), and *Global Chinese* (De Gruyter), and is currently editor of the *International Journal of Bilingual Education and Bilingualism* (Taylor & Francis). His books include the *Blackwell Guide to Research Methods in Bilingualism and Multilingualism* (with Melissa Moyer) and *Translanguaging: Language, Bilingualism and Education* (with Ofelia Garcia), which won the British Association of Applied Linguistics Book Prize.

Zhu Hua
University College London

Zhu Hua is Professor of Language Learning and Intercultural Communication at the UCL Institute of Education, University College London (UCL) and is a Fellow of the Academy of Social Sciences, UK. Her research is centered around multilingual and intercultural communication. She has also studied child language development and language learning. She is book series co-editor for *Routledge Studies in Language and Intercultural Communication* and *Cambridge Key Topics in Applied Linguistics*, and forum and book reviews editor of *Applied Linguistics* (Oxford University Press).

About the Series

Mirroring the *Cambridge Key Topics in Applied Linguistics*, this Elements series focuses on the key topics, concepts and methods in Applied Linguistics today. It revisits core conceptual and methodological issues in different subareas of Applied Linguistics. It also explores new emerging themes and topics. All topics are examined in connection with real-world issues and the broader political, economic and ideological contexts.

Cambridge Elements ⁼

Applied Linguistics

Elements in the Series

Printed in the United States
by Baker & Taylor Publisher Services